D1391816

The Observer's Pocket Series
DOGS

The Observer Books

A POCKET REFERENCE SERIES

COVERING NATURAL HISTORY, TRANSPORT

THE ARTS ETC

Natural History

BIRDS
BIRDS' EGGS
BUTTERFLIES
LARGER MOTHS
COMMON INSECTS
WILD ANIMALS
ZOO ANIMALS
WILD FLOWERS
GARDEN FLOWERS
FLOWERING TREES
                AND SHRUBS
CACTI
TREES
GRASSES
FERNS
COMMON FUNGI
LICHENS
POND LIFE
FRESHWATER FISHES
SEA FISHES
SEA AND SEASHORE
GEOLOGY
ASTRONOMY
WEATHER
CATS
DOGS
HORSES AND PONIES

Transport

AIRCRAFT
AUTOMOBILES
COMMERCIAL VEHICLES
SHIPS

The Arts etc

ARCHITECTURE
CATHEDRALS
CHURCHES
HERALDRY
FLAGS
PAINTING
MODERN ART
SCULPTURE
FURNITURE
MUSIC
POSTAGE STAMPS

The Observer's Book of
DOGS

Edited by
S. M. LAMPSON

DESCRIBING OVER 230
BREEDS AND VARIETIES
WITH 149 ILLUSTRATIONS

FREDERICK WARNE & CO LTD
FREDERICK WARNE & CO INC
LONDON: NEW YORK

Revised edition
© *Frederick Warne & Co. Ltd.*
London, England
1970

Reprinted 1972

LIBRARY OF CONGRESS CATALOG CARD
No. 66–15686

ISBN 0 7232 0090 4

Printed in Great Britain by
William Clowes & Sons, Limited,
London, Beccles and Colchester
1989.272

Contents

Preface

Since writing the last preface five years ago many alterations have taken place in the ever-changing world of dogs. Breeds then hardly known in Great Britain or the United States are now quite familiar. Every effort has been made to give an illustrated description of every breed on the registers of the English and American Kennel Clubs as well as the most frequently seen Continental breeds. Notes on rare, curious and less familiar varieties of dog will be found in the second half of the book.

Once again I thank all those who have taken so much trouble to help me with the information and photographs without which there would be no book.

Dorset, 1970   S. M. LAMPSON

Acknowledgements

In preparing the 1970 edition of this book I have received much help from many dog lovers in many countries, also Mr C. A. Binney of the Kennel Club, to whom I am deeply grateful. Without illustrations the book would be nothing, so to all those who have supplied photographs of their dogs and to the photographers I say a sincere 'thank you': to Mrs D. Albin for the photograph reproduced on page 142; Charles Atkins (Photography) Ltd, 26; Mrs Birchall, 88; Mr and Mrs J. J. Blake, 42; Miss N. Boor, 25; Lilian Brandi, 1; William Brown, 17; Mrs D. Bushby, 76; Miss J. Cameron, 73; Mr D. Campbell, 59; Helen B. Case and Mary Twomey, 69; C. M. Cooke and Son, 3, 5, 29, 41, 43, 51, 53, 54, 64, 67, 78, 105, 110, 112, 113, 127, 129, 138, 148; Mrs M. M. Dod, 2; Thomas Fall, Ltd, 6, 12, 13, 14, 21, 22, 23, 30, 31, 34, 36, 39, 40, 44, 57, 58, 71, 72, 75, 80, 82, 83, 84, 85, 91, 93, 97, 101, 102, 103, 104, 107, 111, 114, 123, 125, 128, 130, 132, 133, 134, 146, 149; Mrs Frei-Denver and C. M. Cooke and Son, 37; H. J. Goater, 15, 28, 66, 68, 81, 92; Miss S. Graham Weall and C. M. Cooke and Son, 116; Mr L. Hamilton-Renwick, 109; Mrs R. T. Harris, 48; Miss O. M. Hastings, 86; Hedges, 46, 124; Mrs A. Heery and C. M. Cooke and Son, 32; the late Miss P. Heynes, 62; the late Mrs C. Hick, 119; Irish Field, 70; Mrs Jenkins and Miss Hourihane, 137; Luther-Smith, 48, 50; Miss Mellis, 52; Miss Morrison-Bell, 126; Mrs Frederick H. Murphy, 27; Mr Graham Newell and C. M. Cooke and Son, 138; Mr and Mrs Prince and Sally Anne Thompson, 118; Ralph Robinson, 135, 139; A. J. Rowell, 96; Dr Braxton B. Sawyer and William P. Gilbert, 8; Evelyn Shafer, 7, 9, 19; F. W. Simms, 143; John Slater, 100; Sport and General, 16, 62; Miss D. Steeds, 122; Mrs Steele, 10; Mrs Roger Stenning, 94; Tauskey, 35; Sally Anne Thompson, 20, 24, 60; Thurse, 65; Mrs M. Tomlin, 26; Dr Zoltan Balássy, 89, 90, 117, 140; T. Viney, 141; Guy Withers, 74. Acknowledgement must also be made to Mr Clifford Hubbard, the first editor of *The Observer's Book of Dogs*, without whose vast knowledge of dogs and their history the book would not have existed.

Introduction

It is a quarter of a century since the first Introduction was written for this book. During those twenty-five years great changes have taken place, for not only have dogs become of far wider importance in the lives of the average citizen but breeds that were previously unknown or of extreme rarity have become generally popular, while a few—a very few—breeds have failed to hold the public affection and have become rare, although seldom extinct.

Mr Hubbard, the first editor of this book, was emphatic that one of its main objects was 'to enable the reader to identify one breed from another with as little effort as possible' while giving the most interesting and prominent facts relating to the origin, history and appearance of each variety. With this in view, the present edition describes and illustrates, in the first part of the book, almost all the breeds of dog accepted by the English and American Kennel Clubs, as well as many of the most popular Continental breeds, and briefly describes in the later pages other less well-known dogs. Breeds are classified in groups accepted by the English and American Kennel Clubs and since Cruft's is now such an outstanding event and the supreme winner at this show a subject of international interest, a list of winners from 1928 to 1970 has been included. There is a glossary of terms in common use when speaking of dogs, and a metric conversion table.

It has been suggested that something should be said about the history of the canine race, but the subject is too vast for such a small book. However, there is good reason for saying something about the care and choice of our own dogs under present-day conditions. The first thing that any dog owner must have is a sense of responsibility— a puppy or adult dog is a living and loving creature and cannot be taken into our homes one day and cast out the next. No one is forced to acquire a dog. Before doing so they should be certain that they really want it and that they can provide it with two basic necessities—affection and companionship. It is unkind to keep a dog when all the household is out of the house all and every day. It cannot be wondered at if a dog left alone for hours at a time relieves its boredom by destroying chairs and cushions, scratching at doors or constantly barking. A dog left in a kennel for long, lonely hours is condemned to imprisonment and it is impossible for any animal kept under such conditions to develop any intelligence. This is not to say that a dog can never be left alone—in fact it should be trained that there are occasions when its presence is not required. Provided it has been given the opportunity to relieve itself, has a comfortable sleeping place and fresh water, a dog can fulfil its duty as guardian of the house while its owners are away for several hours.

Having settled that the dog will be able to receive and give companionship, one stumbling block to happy dog-owning has been removed. The next point to settle is what breed of dog is to be our companion for the next ten or twelve years. This is a point worth careful thought for it is most unwise to install a large dog in a tiny flat or acquire a strong and active animal when one's ability to exercise it is limited. There are many small dogs that are just as intelligent and sporting as their larger relations, while being more reasonable in their demands for exercise. If space is plentiful both inside and outside the house then there are no limits to one's choice. Remember, however, that tiny cuddly puppies at six weeks can be lumbering great hoydens at six months.

The feeding of dogs is, on the whole, easier although more expensive than it used to be. It is no longer possible to nourish a dog on kitchen scraps and plate waste. On the other hand, there are many excellent dog foods available. Adult dogs generally do best on a half-and-half mixture of wholemeal biscuit meal and meat which can be cooked or raw and given either once or twice a day, but always at regular times. Most dwellers in rural areas can get meat from the local slaughter house, and in most towns there are pet shops who supply this type of meat at prices lower than those of a butcher's shop. There are many brands of tinned and frozen dog meats that are useful as a stand-by at holiday time or when travelling by car.

A puppy's diet is rather different and must contain raw meat, but when taking delivery of the puppy from the breeder make certain that you are given detailed instructions on how it has been fed and how often. Carrying on the same methods for the next few days will greatly help the transition in the puppy's life. Afterwards one can gradually increase the quantities and decrease the number of meals until the pup is about one year old and can be considered an adult. The correctly and regularly fed puppy or dog is the one that is easiest to house-train.

There is another important duty to every dog— inoculations against 'hard pad' and other far from rare infections and contagious diseases. Two injections will usually cover these and a veterinary surgeon should be consulted immediately a new dog joins the family, unless it is known for certain that steps have already been taken to immunise him. Even then annual 'booster' injections are often advised.

Yet another consideration—do you want a dog or a bitch? This is purely a matter of personal choice but if it is a bitch that is favoured, remember that she will come 'in season' for about three weeks twice a year from the time she is approximately nine months old. During that period she will be attractive to dogs and she must be confined in a safe but comfortable place where no dog can get to her. It is a fallacy that every bitch must have at least one litter in the course of her life for the good of her health. However, it is true that having a dog castrated or a bitch spayed can put an end to their sexual urges, but if it is done to a young animal solely for this purpose, it is a confession of laziness by the owner and the result usually is a fat, lethargic dog who loses a great deal of its character and charm.

Lastly, no dog or bitch should ever be turned out of the house to exercise itself and should never, under any circumstance, be allowed off a lead on any road, for an accident can happen in a second. And if a human being or the dog dies or is injured through neglect of the animal, it is then too late to be sorry.

Affenpinscher

Monkey Dog

The gay and quaint little Affenpinschers have been known on the Continent for four or five hundred years, although by varying breed names. Today Affenpinschers have gained official acceptance and many friends in the United States, but very little attempt has been made to popularise them in England, possibly because without cropped ears much of their characteristic alert expression might be lost.

The smaller the size of an Affenpinscher the better and $10\frac{1}{2}$ lb is the highest acceptable weight. Nevertheless a sturdy, vivacious dog is required with a round head and large dark eyes. The muzzle to be short, pointed with slightly under-shot jaws and black nose. The coat harsh and wiry but shaggy around eyes, nose and chin, giving the characteristic monkey-like appearance. Ears cropped to a point; tail docked. Black or black and tan are favoured colours but red or grey accepted.

Afghan Hound

These native hounds of Afghanistan are one of the oldest branches of the Greyhound family. Rock carvings at Balkh, dating from the 4th millennium B.C. show similar hounds. The first recorded importation to Britain was 'Shalizada' in 1894. Many descend from the seven imported in 1920 by Major and Mrs Bell Murray and from Mrs Amps' 'Sirdar of Ghazni'. Very popular in Europe and America.

The height should be 27–29 in. The coat may be of any colour and is long and silky except along the saddle where it is short and close. The proudly carried head is crowned with a profuse top-knot. The feet are large and hairy; the tail, carried in a ring, is raised when in action.

Airedale Terrier

Bingley Terrier; Waterside Terrier;
Wharfedale Terrier

The largest of the Terrier family, taking its name from the valley of the Aire, Yorkshire. Created in the middle of last century probably from crossing the Otterhound and black and tan wire-haired sporting Terriers. It was used for tackling vermin, not excluding otters, along the river banks. Popular for its affectionate nature, intelligence and guarding ability.

Height 23–24 in., bitches a little less. The colour of head, ears and legs up to elbows and thighs should be tan and the body black or dark grizzle. Coat harsh, dense and wiry, not too long. Head fairly long with flat skull; ears small and V-shaped; back short and level; legs heavily boned and straight, with compact feet; tail docked, set high and carried gaily.

Akita

Akitas are an ancient Japanese breed of the Spitz family and often used for guard and army purposes although they make excellent sporting dogs. The breed has made little impact in England although a brace was imported in 1937 and one was exhibited at Cruft's in 1959. In the United States the breed is arousing interest although not officially recognised. Since there is no supreme authority on canine matters in Japan information is hard to obtain.

A typical Spitz in appearance with wedge-shaped skull, prick ears, stiff 'fur' on back but softer hair elsewhere. Colour white (except army dogs), fawn, wheaten, black, grey, brindle and black and tan. Akita-Inu stand approx. 20–27 in.; Nippon-Inu 17–21½ in. and have curled, gay and bushy tails, and are often used as sporting dogs; Shiba-Inu stand 14–16 in. and have stumpy or bob tails.

Alaskan Malamute

The Alaskan Malamute and the Husky should not be confused although they are much alike and both are sledge dogs. The Malamute was, in the past, the respected servant of the Mahlemut tribe. When Alaska was settled by the white races the Malamute sledge dog was valued above all others for its remarkable powers of endurance, intelligence, fortitude and memory. These dogs proved their worth on the Arctic and Antarctic expeditions to the Poles. Many are now kept as companions in both England and America.

Height 23–25 in. Weight 75–85 lb. Body strong and compactly built but not unduly short-coupled. Good bone and powerful muscles essential. Thick, dense, double coat. Good ruff around neck. Colour any shade of grey to black, with white under body and on legs. Mask-like markings on face. Plumed tail carried over back.

Alsatian (G.S.D.)

German Shepherd Dog; Schäferhund

This breed only came into existence in its present form about 1899 when Rittmeister von Stephanitz supervised the inter-breeding of three ancient strains of European shepherds' dogs. The result combined beauty and brains. By the early 1920s they were in great demand in Great Britain and the U.S.A. and at the present time are one of the most popular breeds in the world, esteemed for their 'incorruptibility, discernment and ability to reason'. Alsatians are used by the Police, the Services and as Guide Dogs for the Blind.

Height 24–26 in. The smooth, double coat may be of any colour although white is undesirable. The body is long, strongly boned and muscular. The head is long with upstanding ears. The tail hangs in a slight curve.

American Cocker Spaniel

In the U.S.A. the Cocker Spaniel has been developed into a dog of entirely different type and size from the more familiar Cockers of England, the Americans being considerably smaller and having a round skull and a profuse coat which is much barbered for the show ring. Some years ago these pleasant-natured dogs were the most popular breed in the U.S.A. and are still favoured by many as pets but there are few left with working ability. The breed was introduced into England a few years ago and granted its own breed register and championship status in 1970.

Weight from a minimum of 22 lb to a maximum of 28 lb. Eyes round, dark and full. The flat or slightly wavy coat is soft and dense, with profuse feathering on ears, chest, abdomen and legs. Colours black, black and tan, or any solid colour, also parti-colour and roan.

American Foxhound

It is said that a pack of English hounds travelled to America as long ago as 1650. Further Foxhounds crossed the Atlantic in 1742 and 1770, one of the subscribers for the latter draft being George Washington who also received French hounds from Lafayette. In England foxhounds hunt as a pack, but this is not always so in America where individuals are used as 'trail' hounds or raced in pairs on a drag. The result is that although there is a strong resemblance between English and American Foxhounds they are clearly different breeds.

Height 22–25 in., bitches slightly less. Skull fairly long, slightly domed; muzzle of fair length. Ears set on moderately low, long and nearly reaching the tip of the nose when drawn out. Tail set high and carried gaily. Coat close, hard and of any hound colour.

American Water Spaniel

The forefathers of the American Water Spaniel have never been definitely identified, but appearances lead one to believe that Irish Water Spaniels and Curly-coated Retrievers were mainly concerned. Nevertheless, these excellent working spaniels have bred true for many generations. Until their recognition by the American Kennel Club in 1940, these dogs did not appear on the show bench, where they are now quite a familiar sight; but it is as efficient and intelligent gundogs with great enthusiasm for working in water that these dogs are mainly valued in the U.S.A. The breed is still unknown in Britain.

Height 15–18 in. at shoulder and weight 25–45 lb. Skull rather broad and muzzle square; long, wide, lobular ears set on above level of eyes. Coat closely curled or wavy and very dense. The legs have medium-length curly feathering. Colour solid liver or dark chocolate.

Anatolian (Karabash) Dog

These handsome dogs of Mastiff descent are used by Anatolian shepherds to protect their flocks from wolves. In Turkey these dogs have their ears cropped and wear heavy spiked iron collars as protection. The first pair was imported to Britain in 1966 by Mrs C. Steele and exhibited at Cruft's. Other importations followed and litters have been bred. There are now about twenty-five of these dogs in Great Britain and a club has been formed. Not yet known in the U.S.A.

Height 26–30 in. Must be active and powerful with a long, strong back and deep square chest. Head large with broad skull and drop ears. Tail long and carried low with curled end when at rest, but raised over back in action. Coat short and dense, cream to fawn or striped brindle with black mask and ears.

Appenzell Mountain Dog

Appenzell Sennenhund

Of the Swiss Mountain Dogs the Appenzell, named after the Canton of Appenzell, is the second favourite and third in the scale of size. The breed was first introduced into England in 1936 by Mr Mark Welch, who imported a brace from the Appenzell Canton, but interest was not sustained. The Appenzell has boasted a Specialist Club since 1906 and great interest is taken, by breeders and farmers in particular, to maintain a good type. It is used mostly as a herder's or drover's dog.

Height 19–23 in. Weight 32–35 lb. Colour a tricolour of jet black, deep russet brown and clean white. Coat short and dense, flat and shiny. Ears triangular and folded over; body cobby; tail curled tight over the back. (*See* Swiss Mountain Dog.)

Australian Terrier

A fairly popular dog in Australia and New Zealand is the Australian Terrier, which is a low-set dog, showing its descent from the Yorkshire, Norwich, Cairn and other British Terriers, which together made this comparatively recent breed. Although the breed has had many devotees in the Antipodes and has been known there since about 1860, it is still not bred as meticulously as it might be. In fact, many of the British-bred stock are finer in type. Sydney Silky dogs are frequently crossed with Australians, to the disadvantage of both. The breed was introduced to Britain in 1903, and thanks to the pioneering work of the Countess of Stradbroke and Mrs Bassett, it has become well known in England, the U.S.A. and several other countries.

Height 10 in. Weight 10–11 lb. Colour blue or silver-grey on body with tan on legs and face, alternatively sandy or red. Coat straight and hard. Ears pricked or dropped forward; tail docked short.

Basenji

A breed native to the inner Congo basin.
Egyptian rock-carvings of 4000–5000 years ago
depict dogs very similar to the Basenji of today.
The Basenji has many relations, similar in general
build, scattered through the Sudan and Upper Nile.
The Kiljongo natives use them for hunting antelope
and beating big game from their hide-outs, tying
bells and gourds filled with pebbles round the dogs'
necks in order to make as much din as possible.
Mrs O. Burns imported five of the breed into
England in 1936 and since then the Basenji has
become very popular. First imports into the
U.S.A. from Africa took place in 1937.

Height about 17 in. Weight 21–25 lb. Colour
bright red, pure black or black and tan with white
markings. Coat short and smooth. Ears erect;
wrinkled forehead; back short; tail curled tight.
Usually unable to bark but it 'yodels'.

Basset Hound

Little is known of the origin of the Basset Hound, but it is generally accepted that its place of origin was the Artois department of France. They were first mentioned by name in 1585. The finest specimens for some time, however, have reached us from the Vendée district. In Britain the Couteulx strain has been mostly adopted, for the Lane type (light in bone, lemon and white and rather a plain dog) has never found favour; neither has the rough-coated variety. First imported to Great Britain in 1866 by Lord Galway, the Basset was recognised by the Kennel Club in 1883. Now very popular in England and the U.S.A.

Height 13–15 in. Any recognised hound colour is acceptable. The coat is smooth and the skin very loose. The head and velvety ears have a resemblance to those of the Bloodhound; body muscular and of fair length; tail sickle-shaped.

Beagle

The origin of the Beagle is obscure. Queen Elizabeth I hunted with Beagles and Shakespeare mentioned them. Their work has always been the hunting of the hare and there are numerous packs throughout the country. Recently the breed has become popular as companions. For some time Beagles were the most popular breed in the U.S.A. where the original stock had been imported from England. A considerable amount of fresh blood has recently been imported into Britain from the U.S.A., where a smaller hound is preferred.

Height 13–16 in. Coat smooth and short; of any recognised hound colour. Head of fair length with deep muzzle and long, low-set ears. Body short and strong with powerful loins. Tail moderately long and carried gaily.

Bearded Collie

An old and handsome type of working cattle- and sheepdog that, not so long ago, was in grave danger of dying out. Mrs G. O. Willison was largely responsible for seeking out typical stock and arousing interest in a breed that has great sagacity and charm of character. The breed is now well established again in Great Britain where it has trebled its registrations in the past six years. So far it has not been accepted in the U.S.A.

Height 18–24 in. Colour, slate or reddish fawn preferred, but black, all shades of grey, brown and sandy permissible; with or without white markings. The coat is double—the under soft and close and the outer hard, strong and shaggy with definite 'beard' on muzzle.

Bedlington Terrier

Rothbury Terrier

The Bedlington is hardly the sort of dog one could forget if once seen, looking very much like a lamb with its fleece and shape. The origin of the breed is obscure, but it developed in Northumberland and is akin to other terriers of the Border counties—such as the Dandie Dinmont—all of whom were game and sporting. The name Bedlington was first applied in 1825. A dog called 'Old Flint', born in 1782, was one of the early progenitors of the breed, which was then shorter on the leg and lighter in build.

Height 15–16 in. Weight 18–23 lb. Colour blue, blue and tan, liver, liver and tan, or sandy. Coat thick and linty with a tendency to twist. Head and skull narrow but deep and rounded. Profuse silky top-knot. Low-set ears with a fringe at tip.

17

Bernese Mountain Dog

Bernese Sennenhund

These very handsome Swiss dogs are accepted in most countries of Europe and in the U.S.A., but have not yet become established in Great Britain although an importation was made in 1937. The Bernese Mountain Dog descends from the dogs introduced into Helvetia by the Roman legions for guarding their military outposts. Subsequently it became commonplace in the canton of Berne to see these dogs drawing carts in which basket makers and weavers took their goods to market. Today they are seldom used as draught dogs but are valued as companions and houseguards. A specimen of the breed appeared at Crufts in 1972.

Height 23–27½ in. Colour jet black with russet brown or tan markings on legs and over eyes; white chest. Coat long, soft and silky.

Black and Tan Coonhound

These hounds are an American production and are unlikely to be seen outside the U.S.A. Their ancestors probably include Bloodhounds and the black and tan Virginia Foxhounds. Originally intended for tracking raccoon and opossum, they are also used for deer, bear and other game. They track their quarry entirely by scent, and once it is found or treed give tongue until the guns arrive. They are not expected to kill.

A strong, agile dog with powerful and rhythmic movement. Height 23–27 in. Well-developed flews. The ears, low and well set back, hang in folds and should extend well beyond the tip of the black nose. Strong muscular body and straight legs. Coat short and dense. Colour coal black with rich tan on muzzle, over eyes and on chest, legs and breechings. Low-set tail but when dog is in action carried at right-angle to back.

Bloodhound

Sleuth Hound; Slot Hound

The Bloodhound descends from an old breed introduced into England from Normandy by William the Conqueror and used successively as a hunting dog for red deer by William Rufus, patrol dog by the mediaeval curfewmen and later as a tracking dog by the Police. Trained dogs have been known to follow trails over 100 hours old with success. Not often used for tracking criminals now, these hounds are still trained and trials are held.

Height about 26 in. Weight about 80–110 lb. Colour black and tan, red and tan, or tawny. Coat short and glossy. Head large with prominent peak and ample wrinkle, furnished with much loose skin; ears long, set low and pendant; eyes show the 'haw'; tail long and tapering.

Border Terrier

Reedwater Terrier

Most of the breeds common to the north of England are so closely related that it is difficult to say which is descended from which; the Border Terrier might well be the product of the Dandie Dinmont and the Bedlington, yet it might have been the ancestor of one of these breeds. It appears that the breed was known at the end of the 17th century as a sporting dog in Cumberland, Westmorland and Northumberland. Officially recognised by the English Kennel Club as of breed status in 1920 (the American Kennel Club followed suit in 1932), it is a game and sporting dog which is very popular.

Weight 13–15½ lb, bitches 11½–14 lb. Colour red, wheaten, grizzle and tan, or blue and tan. Coat harsh, weather-proof and with a good thick undercoat.

Borzoi

Russian Greyhound; Russian Wolfhound

This is the most elegant and spectacular breed of all dogs. A great favourite with the Russian Court and nobles, the Borzoi was condemned and kennels dispersed when the Bolsheviks came to power. The breed was bred exclusively for the purpose of wolf-hunting. The Borzoi arrived in England about 1875 and immediately attracted attention; many of the leading breeders took an interest in its British future, and by 1892 the first specialist club was formed, largely through the help of the late Duchess of Newcastle. Today, it is bred more for beauty than for coursing, but proves fairly popular in Britain and the U.S.A.

Height not less than 29 in. Coat long and silky, flat, waved or curly. Colours not defined. Head long and fine, deep powerful jaws.

Boston Terrier

This American breed is named after the Massachusetts town and was produced from crossing English and French Bulldogs, plus some Old English Terrier blood. A seal-brindled dog named 'Judge', weighing about 30 lb, was taken to Boston from Liverpool about 1875 and sold to a Mr Hopkin there; this dog later became the founder type. Undoubtedly the smartest and most popular dog of American creation. Some excellent specimens are in Britain now, the smaller being preferred.

Weight 15–25 lb. Colour brindle and white (the white to be on the front, collar and blaze), black and white permissible. Coat short and sleek. Head broad and round; ears erect, rather large; body compact; tail straight or screw.

Bouvier des Flandres

The Bouvier is a dog of rugged appearance whose original work was cattle droving and sometimes sheep herding for Flemish farmers. These dogs first appeared on the show bench in Brussels in 1910 but this attempt to standardise and polish the breed came to an end with the outbreak of war in 1914. About 1920 renewed and more successful efforts were made and the breed can be seen at many Continental shows and is accepted in the U.S.A.

Height 23½–27½ in., bitches less. A compact, powerfully built dog with an intelligent expression. Ears cropped and tail docked to 4 in. Coat rough and wiry and unkempt in appearance but thoroughly weather resisting, the hair on the head forms eyebrows, a moustache and beard. Colours from fawn to black; pepper and salt, grey or brindle.

Boxer

'Flocki', shown at Munich in 1895, the result of a cross made in Germany between a bitch of a bull-fighting type and a Bulldog called Tom, aroused an increasing interest in this new breed, inexplicably called 'Boxers'. The Boxer first went to the U.S.A. about 1903 without making much impact; it was 1911 before one appeared in England and the 1930s before real interest was aroused in either country. Little progress was made in England until 1945. Enthusiasts imported from both America and Germany, and today our best dogs can hold their own in any company. Of moderate size, great strength and activity the Boxer makes a good guard and affectionate companion.

Height 21–24 in. The short, smooth coat is either brindle or fawn often combined with white markings. The head is broad with a deep short, square muzzle and dark mask.

Briard

Berger de Brie

These handsome French herding dogs are a very ancient breed said to have been favoured by the Emperor Charlemagne. It is possible that the Marquis de Lafayette may have been responsible for taking the first Briards to America, but the breed died out. It was after the First World War that returning American troops re-introduced the breed and it is now firmly established. There is a growing interest in these wise and intelligent dogs in England and several appear at the leading shows.

Height 22–27 in. In the U.S.A. ears may be cropped or left natural, in Britain always natural. The heavy hair on the head falls forward to form eyebrows over the intelligent dark eyes. A lithe, well-proportioned square body with muscular limbs. Coat long, slightly wavy, stiff and profuse. Any colour permissible except white. Double dewclaws on hind-legs essential.

Brittany Spaniel

Epagneul Breton

Although an old breed, with a greater resemblance to a setter than a spaniel, the Breton Spaniels fell on hard times and became very degenerate. It was in the present century that it was restored by the careful use of various crosses of Continental sporting dogs such as the Italian Bracco and the Braque de Bourbonnais. The result is an excellent, fast working and intelligent gundog that has travelled from France to make a name for itself in the U.S.A.

A compact, energetic and squarely built dog weighing between 30–40 lb. Height $17\frac{1}{2}$–$20\frac{1}{2}$ in. Coat dense, flat or wavy—never silky—with little feathering. Colour dark orange and white or liver and white. Nose brown or deep pink. Tail approx. 4 in. long, sometimes natural, otherwise docked.

Bull Terrier

The Bull Terrier is the gladiator of the canine race. It is active, strongly built and courageous but of even temperament and amenable to discipline. As its name suggests, it has Bulldog blood in its veins, and the old smooth Black and Tan Terrier and Old English White Terrier were probably relations. The original Bull Terrier was the Bill Sykes tyke of the pits and the rat haunts, but mainly through the efforts of Mr James Hinks, who created the all-white dog of the late 1850s, the breed has now become the companion of discriminating dog-lovers all over the world. Its popularity is world-wide, and exports from Britain to the U.S.A. and to India are numerous.

There are neither weight nor height limitations but the maximum substance for the size of dog is required. Colour pure white, or white with markings on the head, or 'coloured', i.e. brindle or black to predominate. Coat short and smooth.

Bull Terrier (Miniature)

The attempt to breed perfect Bull Terriers in miniature has been going on for a long time and has proved surprisingly difficult. The limited number of typical specimens that are bred have a tremendous charm of both appearance and character for they have a great sense of fun as well as being extremely affectionate, courageous and intelligent. If more of them were to appear before the general public they would become more popular. The English Kennel Club recognises them as a separate breed.

The standard for the Bull Terrier (Miniature) is as that of its larger relation with the exception that the height must be not more than 14 in. and the weight must not exceed 20 lb. The smaller the better, providing type and substance are retained.

Bulldog

Bull-baiting Dog; Old English Bulldog

The Bulldog is considered the national British breed and typifies tenacity, determination and courage. We first hear of a bull being baited by dogs in 1209. This unpleasant so-called sport flourished until abolished by law in 1835.

The appearance of the modern Bulldog is of a smooth-coated, thick-set dog of rather low stature although broad, powerful and compact. The head is strikingly massive in proportion to the size of the dog. In nature Bulldogs are docile and affectionate.

Weight 50–55 lb. Any colour except black or black and tan, or dudley (yellow). Jaw undershot; chops deep; ears 'rose' set high; body roach-backed, deep-chested with tucked up belly.

Bullmastiff Keepers Night Dog

As a breed the Bullmastiff is comparatively new, but it is true to say that Bulldog-Mastiff crossbred dogs have been used for a century or so by gamekeepers of large estates. Since then the breed has become established into a defined type and is becoming increasingly popular as a guard and companion dog. The temperament of the breed combines high spirits, reliability, activity, endurance and alertness. In 1924 the English Kennel Club gave it official recognition. Since the American Kennel Club recognised the Bullmastiff in 1934 the breed has made good headway in the U.S.A.

Height 25–27 in. Weight 110–130 lb, bitches 90–110 lb. Colour any shade of red, fawn or brindle with a dark mask. Coat short and dense. Head large and square; body short-backed; tail thick at set-on, tapering to a point.

Cairn Terrier

This small working Terrier, developed in the Hebrides and Western Highlands, is probably descended from the same parent stock as the Scottish Terrier, Skye Terrier and West Highland White Terrier, and has changed little since the end of the last century. Keenly alert, the Cairn has a foxy or varminty expression quite in keeping with its fearless and gay disposition. Its original work was to 'rout out foxes, badgers, martens and wild-cats from their dens'.

Height 10 in., bitches 9½ in. Weight 14 lb. Colour, any shade except white accepted, but red, wheaten, fawn and light brindle preferred; all show dark masks. Coat profuse and harsh with close furry undercoat. Head foxy with strong jaws; ears small, pointed and erect; back strong and level; legs well boned with strong hind-quarters; tail short and carried gaily.

Catalan Sheepdog

Gos D'Atura; Perro de Pastor Catalán

A Spanish Sheepdog common to Catalonia and used as a cattle-drover as well as a herder. It is very similar to a small Old English Sheepdog and has probably descended from the Pyrenean Mountain Dog. The Real Sociedad Central de Fomento de las Razas Caninas en España (a body equivalent to the English Kennel Club and affiliated to the Fédération Cynologique Internationale) has done much to improve the breed, but it is not yet well known outside Spain.

Height 18–20 in., bitches 17–19 in. Weight 40–45 lb, bitches 36–40 lb. Colour, black and white, grey, russet or black, white and tan; white on whole-coloured dogs is undesirable. Coat long, off-standing and slightly wavy. Head broad and large; ears pendant and set low; back rather short with deep chest; feet large; tail often docked to a maximum of 4 in.

Cavalier King Charles Spaniel

In 1926 Mr Roswell Eldridge of New York announced that he would award £25 in each of two classes at Cruft's Show for 'Blenheim Spaniels of the Old Type as shown in pictures of Charles II's time'. There were only two competitors but interest increased and by 1928 the Cavalier King Charles Spaniel Club had been formed. Although much King Charles Spaniel blood was used, a very different type of toy spaniel soon emerged with a differently shaped skull and longer muzzle. These 'Cavaliers' are now extremely popular since they are active, sporting and intelligent. Not yet acknowledged by the American Kennel Club.

Weight 10–18 lb. Coat long, silky and free from curl with feathering on legs, ears and tail. The skull almost flat between the high set ears; length from stop to tip of nose about 1½ in. Muzzle tapered to a point.

Chesapeake Bay Retriever

American Duck-Retriever

In 1807, an English brig foundered off the Maryland coast—the crew and two puppies were rescued by the American ship *Canton*. The puppies, named 'Canton' and 'Sailor', one black and the other 'dingy red', were probably of the breed that produced the modern Labrador retriever; remaining in the locality they became excellent gun and water dogs. From this pair descended a line of hardy dogs noted for their prowess in the icy waters of Chesapeake Bay. Crosses of other retrieving breeds may have been made in later years. The Chesapeake Bay retriever is recognised by the American Kennel Club but there are now one or two specimens in Great Britain.

Height 21–26 in. Weight 65–75 lb. The coat is thick, short and wavy and the harsher outer coat somewhat oily and thus resistant to wet. The colour varies from dark brown to 'dead-grass'.

Chihuahua (Smooth Coat)

Mexican Dwarf Dog; Ornament Dog;
Pillow Dog

A diminutive breed of Mexican origin and developed in the U.S.A. and now one of the most popular toy breeds in both America and Great Britain. Chihuahuas are said to descend from the sacred dogs of the Aztecs. The noble families are said to have often kept upwards of a thousand dogs each with its attendant slave. Today they are alert, hardy little dogs and their large upstanding ears add to the impression of intelligence.

The smaller the size of the dog the better, providing type is retained but weight should never be above 6 lb. The coat is of fine, close texture and of any colour. The flat furry tail is of medium length and carried up or over the back.

Chihuahua (Long Coat)

The long-haired Chihuahua is basically of the same make and shape as the smooth-haired variety and both types sometimes appear in the same litter. Since 1964 the two coat varieties have divided into separate breeds in Great Britain. It is possible that the appearance of the longer coat could be attributed to a very distant connection with the Papillon, to which breed there is a slight resemblance.

The size and colours of the long-coated variety are the same as for the smooth coats but the coat is longer and silky but quite flat on the body, whilst the ears, fore-legs, hind-quarters and tail are slightly fringed. Although so small and dainty all Chihuahuas should have a brisk, forceful action.

Chinese Crested Dog

Although of Chinese origin, these almost hairless dogs are now rare in their native land. However, they are being bred in the U.S.A. and a few are appearing at English shows. Although unlikely to have a universal appeal, these little dogs are lively and affectionate.

Height about 13 in. Weight 15–18 lb. Colour pink or white, with red or blue flecks or spots, slate blue, blue mottled, pied and all white. There is a tuft of long hair on the skull, 'socks' above the feet and a tuft on the end of tail. Ears large and erect.

Chow Chow

A Chinese breed, the Chow Chow dates back
several thousand years. A typical Spitz with the
short back, cobby build, pointed and erect ears,
and curled tail, it was bred for centuries for its fur
and flesh, and is still so bred in Mongolia. The
breed has a peculiar bluish-black tongue. It was
first mentioned in England in 1789. This attractive breed is now popular in England and the
U.S.A. Being aloof and suspicious it is an excellent guard, although devoted to its owners.

Height not less than 18 in. Colour red, black,
blue, fawn, cream or white. Coat abundant,
dense and with a stand-off ruff, profuse mane and
thick undercoat. A smooth-coated variety is seen
occasionally. Head has a flat, broad skull; ears
small, erect; body compact; legs straight; tail well
plumed and carried over the back.

Clumber Spaniel

The largest of the English sporting Spaniels, and named after Clumber Park, where it was developed about 1770. Of French origin, the breed's antecedents are mysterious; the 'Alpine Spaniel' has been a suggested relation but little is known of these dogs. Although not the least popular of the Spaniel family, the Clumber Spaniel is by no means well known, despite the great efforts of King George V to resuscitate the breed. Of recent years there has been increasing interest in these excellent working dogs.

Height about 18 in. Weight 55–70 lb. Colour white with lemon markings on ears, head or muzzle; body markings are undesirable. Coat abundant, close, silky and straight; legs well feathered. Head large and round; ears, vine-leaf shaped, hang slightly forward; body long and heavy and near the ground; tail short, well feathered.

Cocker Spaniel

The Cocker Spaniel has proved such a charming and merry companion that it is only a minority of them who are trained to the gun. It is less than a hundred years since the small and shorter-bodied spaniels officially parted company with the Field and Springer spaniels and became Cockers. The flat silky coat may be any of a variety of colours —solid black, red, golden and occasionally liver. There are parti-colours and tricolours, the colour usually broken up with white. There is also a variety of roans. The long, lobular ears covered with silky hair and the short, constantly wagging tail are features of the breed.

Weight is about 25–28 lb. The skull and forehead are sufficiently developed to provide plenty of brain space whilst the muzzle is well developed and square.

Collie (Rough)

Scotch Colley Dog

A widely known Scottish sheep-herding breed of great intelligence and beauty. Its name is probably derived from the colley or mountain sheep of the Scottish Highlands. It is an expert at handling large flocks and popular in Australia for that reason. The breed was very popular in the early years of the century but had a serious decline from which it has only recently recovered.

Height between 20 and 24 in. Colour and markings are immaterial. The coat should be dense and the outer coat harsh to the touch; the mane and frill abundant, moderately long tail never carried over the back. Ears semi-erect when alert.

Collie (Smooth)

The Smooth-haired Collie is a more uncommon variety of the breed, which merits a greater degree of popularity than it has received as yet. It had its own classes at the Darlington Show in 1870, but was seen less and less often until quite recently when quite a number have been exhibited at the leading shows. Merle colouring, together with the 'wall' eye seem more common in this variety than the rough.

Height 22–24 in., bitches 20–22 in. Coat short and smooth but not furry; undercoat dense and thick. (*See* Collie, Rough.)

Curly-coated Retriever

Unfortunately, the curly-coated variety of the Retriever is somewhat uncommon at the present time—although numbers are increasing once more. The late Brig. General Lance did much to ensure the breed's survival. As a sporting dog, it is of immense value, being well disciplined and keen; the tightly curled coat which so often gathered burrs during the day's work was possibly one drawback which caused the Curly to go out of favour. His exact origin is not known, but amongst his ancestors were probably the now extinct Water Dog and, possibly, the Irish Water Spaniel. The Curly has always been a worker rather than a companion dog and a number now appear at shows on both sides of the Atlantic.

Height approximately 22 in. Weight about 70–80 lb. Colour jet black or liver. Coat tight crisp curls from the peak of the head to the set-on of tail; coat is of utmost importance to this breed.

Dachshund (Smooth-haired)

Teckel

Long-bodied, short-legged dogs have been known since the days of Ancient Egypt and remains of dogs of a similar type to the Dachshund have been found in several Romano-Germanic settlements. Nevertheless, it is impossible to claim an unbroken line of descent.

It was the 19th century before Dachshunds became known outside Germany where they were used for badger digging or hunting in packs. During the 1914–18 War there was a senseless antipathy to the breed followed by a rush into popularity immediately afterwards.

Dogs should not exceed 25 lb and bitches 23 lb. Any colour except white acceptable, including dapple. Coat short and smooth. Long, low, muscular body with prominent breast-bone. The fore-legs incline slightly inward and the front feet are full and broad and may incline slightly outward.

Dachshund, Miniature (Smooth-haired)

Kaninchenteckel

The German title for this diminutive Dachshund signifies that the variety is often used for
rabbit hunting. This is significant in that it means
a Miniature Dachshund should be a sturdy little
sportsman, with all the character of its parent stock.
Except for size the Miniature Dachshund is
identical in appearance to its larger relations.
These little dogs have been popular in most parts
of the world for quite a long time and the ugly,
round skulls and pop-eyes, once so often seen have
been eliminated. At shows in the U.S.A. the
miniatures are not treated as separate varieties but
there are classes restricted by weight.

Height about 7–8 in. Chest measurements are
about 11–12 in. in circumference. Weight not to
exceed 11 lb; in the U.S.A. 9 lb. (*See* Dachshund,
Smooth-haired.)

Dachshund (Long-haired)

This long-coated variety of the Dachshund is not yet quite as well known as the Smooth Dachshund, but it would appear to make up for this in the beauty of its coat. Its origin is not known precisely, although it is probably true that a small Setter or Spaniel was bred with the Smooth Dachshund at one time to impart the silky texture to the hair. The Long-haired Dachshund has been mentioned in German records for over 100 years, and exhibited since 1898. It is a good sporting dog and full of character, and since its arrival in England it has become a general favourite with its own specialist Club.

Coat rich and silky, of medium length on the back, but longer on the ears, under the neck and under the entire lower part of the body, with featherings on the legs and long flag to the tail. (*See* Dachshund, Smooth-haired.)

Dachshund, Miniature (Long-haired)

The Miniature Long-haired Dachshund is a gay, bold and alert little dog and despite its small size is strong, active, hardy and very game: in consequence it enjoys considerable popularity. Being very affectionate by nature these little dogs make excellent pets for those who require a small dog but do not favour the toy breeds.

Weight must not exceed 11 lb, but other points being equal, the smaller the dog the better and the ideal weight is 7–9 lb. As with the other varieties any colour is permissible.

Dachshund (Wire-haired)

Although not such a popular variety as the Smooth-haired Dachshund, the Wire-haired type is probably the best suited for working purposes. The slight advantage of having a rough and weather-resisting coat appears to be supported by a remarkable fortitude and adaptability not so apparent in its fellow varieties, and for this reason the Wire-haired Dachshund has been used in wild boar hunting and for beating stag. In 1888 classes were put on for the variety in Berlin, and they proved so successful that by 1927 the Wire-haired Dachshund Club was formed to cater for the Fancy in England. The variety has a slightly more Terrier-like appearance than its cousins.

Weight 18–20 lb. All colours permitted. With the exception of the jaw, eyebrows and ears the body is covered with an even, short, harsh coat and an undercoat. Bearded chin, bushy eyebrows. Smooth hair on ears.

Dachshund, Miniature (Wire-haired)

The Wire-haired Miniature Dachshund is the latest variety of this family to gain the recognition of the English Kennel Club and its popularity is steadily increasing. There is something endearing in the fact that a dog so small can have so much determination and vitality. Like the rest of their family they are most affectionate and faithful to their owners and, since they are so alert, they make excellent little watchdogs.

Weight must not exceed 12 lb; in the U.S.A. 9 lb. In all other respects they are replicas of the Wire-haired Dachshunds.

Dalmatian

Carriage Dog; Coach Dog

The breed first came to England during the 18th century and their splendid physique made them valued as coach dogs. It was originally intended that they should be guards for the mail coaches but, before long, no smart or fashionable equipage was considered complete without one or two of these dogs running either beside the wheels or with their noses to the back axle. The arrival of the internal combustion engine made their task redundant and now these dogs are simply pleasant and sometimes sporting companions.

Weight 50–55 lb. The sleek, glossy coat should be short and fine: the ground colour pure white with round, well-defined spots of black or liver colour. The body spots should be approximately $1\frac{1}{4}$ in. in diameter and smaller on head, face, ears, tail and legs.

Dandie Dinmont Terrier

The Dandie Dinmont Terrier is a very old Border breed. The appearance of Sir Walter Scott's *Guy Mannering* in 1814 was the means of arousing public interest in these dogs, since one of the characters, 'Dandie Dinmont', owned a pack of these sporting terriers. Therefore, it seemed fitting that these tough, working terriers who had become so popular through their appearance in a famous novel should take the breed name of Dandie Dinmont Terriers.

Weight about 18 lb. Height at the shoulder 8–11 in., and the dog's body long, low and muscular. The body coat is crisp but the large, domed head is crowned with soft, silky hair. Body colour may be 'pepper' or 'mustard'.

Deerhound

The Scottish Deerhound is one of the oldest breeds in the British Isles. The failure of the rising in '45 which sent many Scottish chieftains abroad, together with the perfecting of firearms ruined many famous Deerhound strains and the practice of coursing the deer with hounds gave way to the use of the rifle. The purity of the breed would have been lost but for the efforts of a band of enthusiasts. Landseer, Sir Walter Scott and dog shows did a great deal to bring it into the public eye and its popularity is now increasing.

Height not less than 30 in., bitches not below 28 in. Weight 85–105 lb. Colour grey, brindle and wheaten; red, sandy and fawn were once very popular. A thick, close-lying, harsh somewhat ragged coat is required, with a moustache of silky hair. (*See* Irish Wolfhound.)

Dobermann

This German breed came into being from crossing various breeds including early Rottweilers and large black and tan Terriers. It took its name from Louis Dobermann of Apolda, Thuringia, who founded the breed as a type from a bitch named 'Schnupp' in 1890. In or about 1910 Otto Göller also took an active interest in the breed and saved it from threatened extinction. It is much appreciated as a guard and companion dog, and is very popular in Britain, U.S.A. and Africa.

Height 27 in., bitches 25½ in. Colour black, brown or blue with rust markings. Coat short and harsh. Head clean-cut; ears cropped on the Continent but in Britain preferably erect; body lithe and muscular; legs fairly long; tail docked short; the whole dog looking very much like a large Manchester Terrier.

Egyptian Sheepdog

Armant; Ermenti; Sabe

The Egyptian Sheep-
dogs are quite an old
breed native to Upper
Egypt and named
after the hill village
of Armant, where
they are used as sheep-
herders and guards,
having ferocious dis-
positions towards
strangers. Many
Egyptian shepherds
believe them to be
descended from lions,
placing high value on
the dogs. The first
specimens of the
breed to reach Europe
were four owned by

H.E. Prof. Dr Nachât Pasha, when he was the
Egyptian Ambassador to Berlin; on Dr Nachât
transferring his office to England he brought
'Boy', his most typical Armant, with him. This
dog was the only known specimen to have come to
England.

Height 22 in. Weight 50 lb. Colour black,
black and white, tan and white and grizzle and
white, the top-knot, muzzle and brisket to be
white. Coat long and shaggy. The tail is sometimes docked, though it is quite attractive when
left at natural length, hanging low, with an upward
curl at the tip.

Elkhound

Norwegian Elkhound; Graa Dyréhund;
Gráhund

A breed which the casual observer often confuses with the Keeshond is the Elkhound, a Scandinavian elk-hunting dog. A member of the Spitz group, this breed is typically reliable as a bird-, elk- or bear-hunter. It was introduced into Britain in the 1870s, but it hung fire for a while. Later it gathered a band of supporters, until in 1923, when the British Elkhound Society was formed, it became firmly established. The Elkhound, since its recognition by the English and American Kennel Clubs, is very popular on both sides of the Atlantic.

Height 20½ in., bitches 19½ in. Weight 50 lb, bitches 43 lb. Colour grey. Coat abundant, coarse and weather-resisting, short on the face and front of legs, long on the neck, buttocks and backs of fore-legs. Body short and strong; tightly curled tail.

English Foxhound

The modern Foxhound is closely related to the old and now extinct Southern Hounds, the Talbots and the St Huberts of the Ardennes. Fox-hunting is not as old as stag-hunting, but the hound commonly used for that sport has now been stabilised for at least three centuries as a defined type; in the 13th century, hounds were used to the fox, but they were slow plodders compared with the modern dog. In this country the Foxhound is seldom kept as a companion or housedog but kennelled in packs and used solely for fox-hunting. There is a number of English Foxhounds in U.S.A. They are recognised as a separate breed from American Foxhounds (*see* p. 8).

Height approximately 23 in. Weight about 70 lb. Colour tan and white with black markings, tan and black with white legs, throat and tail, lemon and white and pied mixtures. Coat short and smooth.

English Setter

The English Setter combines great physical beauty and charm of character with working ability. Setting dogs were first heard of in this country during the 16th century.

As a breed the English Setters owe a great deal to Mr Edward Laverack and Mr Purcell Llewellin. During the 19th century these men did much to improve their appearance and working ability.

Height $25\frac{1}{2}$–27 in., bitches 24–$25\frac{1}{2}$ in. Weight 60–66 lb, bitches 56–62 lb. The coat should be slightly wavy, long and silky with breeching and fore-legs well feathered. Colours black and white, lemon and white, liver and white, or tri-colour. Scimitar-shaped tail well feathered.

English Springer Spaniel

The Springer Spaniel is one of the oldest branches of the spaniel family tree. Originally spaniels were expected to spring game for the nets or for falcons. Today they find, flush and retrieve for the gun. Although many are seen at shows or kept as companions it is when trained to their natural work that they are seen at their best. The old name of 'Norfolk Spaniel' is now obsolete and the title 'Springer' was officially adopted early in the present century; they are the highest on the leg and raciest in build of all the British land spaniels.

Height about 20 in. Weight 40–50 lb. Colour generally liver and white or black and white, but any spaniel colouring acceptable. Coat close and weather-resisting. A compact, symmetrical and merry dog; very active.

English Toy Terrier (Black and Tan)

Manchester Terrier (Toy)

This is a diminutive Manchester Terrier, for its shape, colour and coat are practically identical with those of its parent type. In the 1870s these little dogs were very popular in London, where the fashionable weight never exceeded 7 lb. Despite being so small these little dogs are true terriers and full of courage and have been known to kill rats as large as themselves. Increasing in popularity. Known in the U.S.A. as Toy Manchester Terriers.

Weight not over 8 lb, though some are as small as 3–4 lb; in the U.S.A. not exceeding 12 lb. Colour black with rich mahogany tan on the muzzle, throat, fore-legs, insides of the hind-legs and under the tail. The coat is smooth, short and glossy. Ears erect or semi-erect.

Entlebuch Mountain Dog

Entlebucher Sennenhund

Smallest of the Swiss quartette of farm, mountain and draught dogs, the Entlebuch breed of Sennenhund is fast approaching a degree of popularity it has never before experienced. The Entlebuch is named after a river flowing through a Lucernese valley, and is easily distinguished from the other three Swiss Mountain Dogs by its not having the full  natural tail; usually wearing a short stump, the Entlebuch is occasionally seen absolutely tailless. It has been bred most carefully from the larger stock, to become the ideal Swiss drovers' dog. The Specialist Club has worked hard and, since the general revival of interest in the breed in 1936, has succeeded in attracting the attention of foreign breeders. In the Netherlands there is now a particularly keen interest in the Sennenhund group.

Height 14–18 in. Weight 20–30 lb. Colour the characteristic tricolour of jet black, deep russet brown and clean white. Coat smooth and short. Tail close-docked or absent.

Field Spaniel

The Field is a British-developed spaniel whose origin is closely linked with that of the Cocker Spaniel. At one time great length of body was a virtue. Since the last century Field Spaniel backs have been shortened and a little weight taken off, until the breed now almost resembles a stoutly built Cocker Spaniel. It has not been a widely favoured breed among shooting-men, although larger than the Cocker and more active than the Clumber. After a very lean period the breed has regained popularity and is represented at leading shows on both sides of the Atlantic.

Height 16–18 in. Weight 35–50 lb. Colour black, liver, mahogany red or roan the most usual, though all colours are permitted. Coat flat, dense and silky. General appearance of a well-balanced, upstanding sporting dog.

Finnish Spitz

Barking Bird Dog; Finnish Cock-eared Dog;
Suomalainen Pystykorva

A typical Northern dog bred in Finland and
Lapland for centuries as a hunting and watch-dog,
the Finnish Spitz is closely related to the Karelian
Spetz and is identified with the forest game of
Northern Scandinavia. It is used mostly for
ranging, finding and pointing capercailzie and
black bird game. The breed was introduced into
England in 1927 by Sir Edward Chichester, and
is now well established. Its courage and fidelity
and intelligent appearance have made it many
friends. Not yet acknowledged in the U.S.A.

Height $17\frac{1}{2}$–20 in. Colour bright reddish brown
or yellowish red on back, lighter on rest of body.
Coat short except on back, back of thighs and tail,
semi-erect on neck. Head foxy, with a sharp
muzzle; ears erect and pointed; back short and
level; tail bushy and curled over the back.

Flat-coated Retriever

Wavy-coated Retriever

Retrievers came into existence in the early 19th century when our ancestors found that they required a dog whose sole purpose was to pick up the game they shot. Various crosses were tried and one that found favour was first called the Wavy-coated Retriever but later this was changed to Flat-coated Retriever. Probably their ancestors were Setters and Spaniels with a later cross with one of the Newfoundland dogs but of which type history does not relate. This breed was very popular for a number of years but later lost ground to the Labrador Retrievers; it is now coming to the fore once more.

Weight about 60–70 lb. Colour black or liver. Coat dense and of fine quality and as flat as possible. An active medium-sized dog of good physique and great intelligence and docility.

Fox Terrier (Smooth)

The smooth-haired variety of Fox Terrier is not quite so popular as their wire-haired relations, despite the fact that they are the senior branch of the family. The general appearance is that of a gay, lively and intelligent little dog. The Fox Terrier Club drew up a Standard of Points for the breed as early as 1876. Breeders have taken considerable care to maintain type and it is very popular in most parts of the world, especially in hot climates.

Weight is not considered a criterion of a dog's fitness for his work but between 15–18 lb is a good average. Colour: white should predominate and black or tan markings are the most usual. Coat short, hard and smooth. Ears V-shaped, small and dropping forwards, close to the cheeks. Tail docked and set on high.

Fox Terrier (Wire)

This is undoubtedly the most well known of all the Terrier family, but it is not quite the general favourite it used to be. Lively and alert, the Wire makes a good companion and house dog.

The breed is still at times used for fox bolting, and should be small enough to enter a fox-earth or drain yet large enough to run with hounds. As a recognised breed the Fox Terrier does not go back so very far, but for several centuries there have been available many writings of earth dogs and 'terrars'; it is to be hoped that the breed will remain game and fearless even though the majority are now kept as companions or for exhibition.

Height about 15½ in. Weight 16–18 lb. Colour predominantly white, usually with black or tan head or body markings; the 'Hound-marked' dog is much admired. Coat dense and wiry; the jaw should be well whiskered.

French Bulldog

Bouledogue Français

Quite distinct in appearance from the English Bulldog is the French version, with its brindle colour and large bat ears. English efforts to breed small but sound bulldogs had failed, so in 1894 Mr Krehl imported several small active bulldogs with upstanding ears from France. These were not well received by English breeders who had been beaten at their own game. However, the French Bulldog Club of England was formed in 1902 and fostered such interest in the breed that by 1910 it had become well established. In America, it reached its heyday during 1900–10.

Weight about 28 lb for dogs and 24 lb for bitches. Colour: all brindles (dark preferred), fawns and pieds. Coat short and fine. Head square and broad; ears large and bat; tail short and thick at the base.

German Shorthaired Pointer

The German Shorthaired Pointers descend from the old slow, heavy Spanish Pointers. The objective was a breed that would be capable of tracking and pointing its game and retrieving it once it had been shot. The German Club to improve and stabilise the young breed was founded in 1872. Americans and Canadians found these 'bird dogs' of value in their type of country and imported a number between 1918 and 1939. In Great Britain a club to further interest in the breed was established in 1951 and a few dogs appeared at shows in 1953. Progress has been steady and they are becoming more popular in the show ring and the field; they are now recognised by the English Kennel Club.

Height 21–25 in. at shoulder. Weight 45–70 lb. Colour either solid liver, liver and white spotted or ticked. Coat short, flat and coarse to the touch. The thick, high-set tail is docked to approximately half-length.

German Wirehaired Pointer

Deutsch-Drahthaar

German breeders have tried hard to produce a perfect working dog which would hunt, point, track and retrieve both game and vermin in any sort of weather. The most successful attempt was made at the end of the last century and produced the Wirehaired Pointer. Great emphasis is placed on the close-lying, straight, harsh, wiry outer coat and dense undercoat which, with considerable furnishings around muzzle and over eyes, are resistant to water, brambles and undergrowth. Sturdy, intelligent and good workers, Wirehaired Pointers first went to the U.S.A. in 1920 and in 1959 they were accepted by the A.K.C. As yet they have made no serious impact in England.

Height 24–26 in., bitches less. Colour liver and white, usually spotted, ticked or roan, but sometimes solid liver. Nose dark brown. Head and ears brown. Tail docked to $\frac{2}{5}$ of original length.

Glen of Imaal Terrier

This small working Terrier of Eire is named after the Glen of Imaal, Co. Wicklow. It is used mostly as a badger-dog, being exceptionally game and of a handy size for entering the pipes. For centuries these dogs have been used in the out-of-the-way dales and glens for fighting purposes, heavy wagers being made on their chances of victory. The sport is now illegal, but the custom at least ensured a tenacity of purpose well fitted for the badger drive. It is officially recognised in Eire, but not elsewhere, and was exhibited for the first time as a distinct breed at the Irish Kennel Club Show, Dublin, in March 1934. A Glen of Imaal must possess the Teastas Misneac (Dead-Game Cert.) before he can become a full Champion.

Height 14 in. Weight 30–35 lb. Colour wheaten, blue, or blue and tan. Coat fairly harsh but untrimmed. Legs short, fore-legs bowed for digging; tail set high and carried gaily.

Golden Retriever

There has always been controversy about the origins of the breed but it is now established that a retriever dog called 'Nous', of uncertain origin, was mated in 1868 to a Tweedside Spaniel bitch, a breed now extinct. At least one of the progeny was mated with an Irish Setter. The Golden Retriever Club was founded in 1911 and the breed rapidly gained popularity after 1918 when its charming character and working ability became appreciated. Very popular in England, America and wherever it goes.

Height about 23 in. Weight 65–70 lb, bitches 55–60 lb. Colour any shade of gold or cream but not red or mahogany. Coat flat or wavy but not curled, with moderate featherings on the fore-legs and tail.

Gordon Setter
Black and Tan Setter

The 4th Duke of Gordon (1743–1827) is usually credited with breeding these black and tan setters; however, from records it would seem that most of the dogs from the Gordon Castle kennel at the time of its dispersal were either black and white or black, white and tan. In the latter half of the 19th century and the early years of the 20th century there was a very active interest in Black and Tan Setters both in this country, the U.S.A. and Scandinavia where they were valued in the field and as show and companion dogs, but the breed has never regained the position it held up to the time of the First World War. In 1924 Gordon Setter was accepted as the official breed title.

Height 26 in. Weight about 65 lb. Colour a deep shining coal black, with bright chestnut markings. Coat straight or slightly wavy but not curly; longer hair on the ears, chest and belly, the legs feathered and the stern flagged.

Great Dane Deutsche Dogge; German Mastiff

During the last three centuries the Great Dane, originally a fighting dog, has become lighter in build, bred for greater speed. From the 17th century it was used for hunting the wild boar in Germany, Denmark and France, and was later introduced into England. These are very elegant dogs with a look of dash and daring. They make excellent guards and companions.

Height a minimum of 30 in. Weight a minimum of 120 lb. Colour brindle, black, fawn and blue; also 'harlequin', a pure white underground with either black or blue patches. Coat short dense and sleek. Head should have medium stop; ears small and set high (cropped on the Continent); body deep, muscular yet graceful; tail carried low.

Greyhound

The Greyhound is one of the most ancient breeds and as a coursing hound was well known to the Greeks and Romans. King Henry VIII was fond of having wagers on these hounds but it was not until the reign of Queen Elizabeth I that the Duke of Norfolk drew up the first rules for coursing. The sport retained its popularity even through the Puritan régime. The Waterloo Cup was first run in 1836. Since 1926 track racing has attracted millions of fans. As a companion and as a show dog the breed is now more popular than it has been for a long time.

Height 28–30 in. Coat short and smooth. Tail long and low set. Colours black, white, red, blue, fawn, fallow or brindle, or any of these colours broken with white.

Griffon Bruxellois

Brussels Griffon; Petit Brabançon

The earliest Griffons were bred by the artisans and cab drivers of Belgium particularly in Brussels. In 1886 the breed made its first show appearance although a dog called 'Vom' came to England in 1880. To improve the breed several crosses were introduced in the early days. It is now one of the most popular of the toy breeds owing to its spirited intelligence and devotion.

Weight most desired between 6 and 9 lb. Colour red, black, or black and tan. The coat of the 'rough' variety harsh and wiry with bearded foreface. Smooth variety (Petit Brabançon) has smooth, close coat. In the U.S.A. black Brabançons are not allowed. Head monkey-like; body compact; tail docked short.

Groenendael

Belgian Shepherd Dog

The best known of the three main types of Belgian shepherds' dogs, and named after the village of Groenendael near Brussels, the Groenendael Sheepdog was recognised as a pure breed by the Belgian Kennel Club in 1891 and imported into England about 1931 by Mrs Grant Forbes, who trained the breed here for general utility work and achieved good results. Belgian farmers and fanciers take great trouble to work the breed, exhibiting being only a secondary activity. The breed is well known in the U.S.A. and achieved championship status in Great Britain in 1971.

Height: average for dogs, 24½ in.; bitches, 23 in. Colour black. Coat long, smooth and straight all over the body with pronounced ruff. Head fairly broad with tapering muzzle; ears triangular, erect and pointing very slightly forwards; body, racy; legs feathered; tail long-haired and set low.

Harrier Hare Hound

The hunting of hares is an even older sport than chasing the fox and it is known that Xenophon (435-354 B.C.) used some form of Harrier in conjunction with the use of nets for hare-catching. Today the net is no longer employed, whilst the dogs are bred taller and faster, a substantial amount of Foxhound blood having been introduced within the last century—a fact which did not necessarily improve the breed. The Harrier is seldom seen on the Show Bench in England, though at Peterborough it is annually exhibited, usually on the day following the Foxhound Show; in America more Harriers are exhibited on the Bench than in the Field. The oldest English pack dates back to 1745, whilst the Welsh Anglesey Harriers trace to 1744.

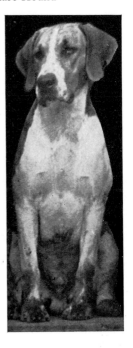

Height 18-19 in.—some packs of doubtful ancestry reach 21-22 in. Colour white with lemon, red, tan or black markings, various pieds and white flecks. Coat short and fairly harsh.

Husky

Eskimo Dog; Sled Dog

The true Husky is the sledge dog bred in West Greenland and Labrador, and should not be confused with other Eskimo varieties. These dogs have outstanding powers of endurance and even in this mechanised age there are many teams of sledge dogs working in snowbound areas where a vehicle cannot penetrate. When allowed to become domesticated Huskies make excellent companions and are very good natured although inclined to be aloof and suspicious with strangers. Undoubtedly very handsome dogs.

Height 21–23½ in. Weight 45–60 lb. The colours are various and often include white on neck, chest and legs. The Husky has a thick, smooth outer coat with a dense downy undercoat. Ears pricked and tail carried over the back. Cap-like mask and spectacles are typical.

Ibizan Hound
Eivissenc; Podenco Ibicenco

The Ibizan Hound is a swift and very ancient type of Greyhound thought to descend from hounds introduced to Ibiza from Egypt by the Moors or the Phoenicians. It has maintained a high degree of purity and is valued as a hunter and watch dog. Two specimens were exhibited at Cruft's in 1929. During the past few years others have been imported and the breed is well on the way to becoming established in England, where a club has been formed. Not yet known in the U.S.A.

Height 22–28 in. Weight 43–50 lb. Colour white and red, white and chestnut, white and lion colour, or any of these colours alone. The coat can be short and smooth or rough and wiry. Body racy with long tail; ears large and erect.

Irish Setter

Red Setter

The early Irish Setters were often red and white but this colouring has died out. The breed has a good reputation as a worker when well trained. After a rather bad patch the breed has now regained its popularity. Elegant and gentle, it is generally like its English cousin in appearance, though differing slightly in head formation and temperament.

The standard for the breed does not state any definite weight or height but these dogs are more racy than those of other Setter breeds. The head is long and lean, the neck long and graceful, the body deep and muscular. The colour is always rich chestnut. The coat flat and silky with feathering on upper ear, back of legs, underparts, tail and between toes.

Irish Terrier

The best known of the Terrier breeds of Ireland. Although these dogs were originally used for sporting purposes they were frequently matched against each other in fights. The breed was first exhibited about 1870 and from then on it became increasingly popular in England and North America. Since the Second World War fewer of these terriers are to be seen around but those who have once owned a 'red devil' are as loyal to their dogs as the dogs are to them.

Height 18 in. Weight 27 lb, bitches 25 lb. Colour red or red-wheaten, though a golden red is becoming popular. Coat hard and wiry. General appearance lithe, wiry and very powerful.

Irish Water Spaniel

The origins of the Irish Water Spaniel are somewhat mysterious but the breed is certainly a very old one. Whether they are in fact true Spaniels is a controversial point. Mr Justin M'Carthy's strain of the 1830s became the type to be established, although several varieties existed in competition. 'Boatswain' was his most notable dog, bred in 1834, and even today the breed has little changed from that time. By no means common, even in its own island, the breed has steadily progressed by sheer hard work on land and water. These dogs are extremely intelligent, and make willing workers, excelling in water retrieving. When 'off duty' they have an endearing and somewhat clownish sense of humour.

Height 21–23 in. Colour rich puce-liver. Coat (the most vital feature) dense, tight and crisp ringlets all over the body except the face, and at tail and front of hind-legs below the hocks.

Irish Wolfhound

A majestic hound of Irish descent, the Irish Wolfhound frequently appears in Celtic legends and history. After the extinction of the wolves the breed degenerated and was almost extinct when about 1860 Captain G. A. Graham devoted himself to the revival of these dogs, using such pure-bred hounds as he could find and making crosses with other large hounds to restore size, stamina and symmetry. Others became interested and the result is the magnificent Wolfhound that we know today.

Height a minimum of 31 in., bitches 28 in. Weight a minimum of 120 lb, bitches 90 lb. Colour grey, brindle, red, black, pure white or fawn. Coat rough and hard. Head long with powerful jaws; ears small; body racy; tail long.

Italian Greyhound

This breed is almost a miniature replica of the Greyhound in its satin-skinned grace and lines. It has been in England from at least the Tudor and Stuart periods. A painting of Queen Anne, wife of James I, now in Hampton Court Palace shows several of this breed. The Italian Greyhound has a characteristic gait entirely its own, not unlike the high-stepping and elegant prance of a prize Hackney pony.

Height 10 in. Weight 6–8 lb. Colours fawn, blue, black, cream, white, or black and fawn and white pied. Coat short, thin and lustrous. Head long, flat and narrow with a fine muzzle; ears rose-shaped; eyes rather large; body racy and tucked-up; legs have very fine bone and a free step; tail set low, long, fine.

Japanese Chin

Chin Chin

A Toy breed distantly related to Pekingese and Pugs. Lee, in his *Modern Dogs*, tells us that the 'Japanese' was exhibited at the Holborn Horse Repository in 1862, whilst it is known that they were on the bench of the Birmingham Show, 1873; thus the Japanese Spaniel was introduced into Britain almost as early as the Pekingese. It has a small but devoted following in England and America, and most European countries.

Height about 10 in. Weight 4–9 lb (above and under 7 lb). Colour white with black, or any shade of red. Coat long, profuse and straight. Head broad, short-nosed and well cushioned; the eyes are large and dark but show the white at the inner corner. Legs light and feathered; tail gay, curled and well plumed.

Keeshond

Dutch Barge Dog

Once familiar sights as they guarded the barges on the Rhine and the Dutch canals. Keeshonds make excellent watchdogs and companions. Isolated examples of the breed appeared in England during the early 19th century but it was early in the present century that Mrs Wingfield Digby brought some puppies over from Holland which aroused great interest. The breed now has many devotees in Great Britain and the U.S.A.

The ideal height is 17–18 in. The body should be short and compact with a fox-like head. The dense, harsh offstanding body coat forms a ruff around the neck but is shorter on head and legs. The eyes have 'spectacles' of lighter hair. The feathered tail curls over the back. Colour wolf or ash grey with cream legs, feet and shadings.

Kerry Blue Terrier

This is the largest of the Irish Terriers native to Eire generally, though revived and popularised mostly by fanciers of Co. Kerry. Probably descended from the Gadhar, an extinct type used by the ancient Irish for sheep herding. The breed began to appear in the English show ring in the early 1920s, since when it has been generally smartened up and become less aggressive. These dogs are loyal and affectionate companions.

Height approx. 18–19 in. Weight 33–37 lb. Colour any shade of blue. Puppies usually darker than adults and may show some tan. Coat soft and wavy, with an abundant forelock. Head long and lean with flat skull and strong jaw and foreface. Body strong, muscular and well proportioned.

King Charles Spaniel

English Toy Spaniel; Spaniel Gentle

There are four varieties of King Charles Spaniels, divided into separate colours, all descended from a common source. The breed is named after Charles II, who, with his brother James II, popularised it, but it existed a good time before that era. In the U.S.A., where a noticeable interest is taken in the breed, it is termed the English Toy Spaniel. The varieties are the Black and Tan or King Charles proper, the Tricolour or Prince Charles, the Ruby and the Blenheim.

Weight 8–14 lb. Colour (King Charles) rich glossy black with bright mahogany tan markings; (Tricolour) white with black patches and tan markings, with white blaze; (Ruby) rich chestnut red; (Blenheim) white with chestnut red patches and wide white blaze, and the famous red spot on the forehead.

Komondor

The Komondor's ancestors are said to have arrived in Europe with the invading Huns. The Magyar herders and shepherds have bred and used Komondor (plural Komondorok) for the protection of the vast herds that range the Puszta and have kept the breed pure. Under working conditions the heavy coat of the breed is allowed to mat, forming a weather proof and protective covering for a dog that is seldom under a roof. When groomed the hair is long on head and body and somewhat ragged or corded. These bold, hardy, tough and independent dogs are seen in many parts of Europe and are fully accepted in the U.S.A., but are not yet seen in England.

The larger the dog the better, with a minimum height of 25½ in. for dogs and 23½ in. for bitches. Colour always white and eyes dark. Tail long and reaching to the hocks but raised to level of the back when the dog is excited.

Kuvasz

The passing of centuries has made it impossible to know the exact origin of the Kuvasz (plural Kuvaszok), but by the 15th century they were the guards and hunting dogs of the Hungarian nobility. King Matthias I (1458–1490) was always accompanied by a Kuvasz upon which he is said to have relied more than his human guards. This monarch kept a large pack of Kuvaszok for hunting purposes, and puppies from his kennels were only given to those the king wished to honour. In later times ownership of these dogs became more general and they were, and still are, much used by the shepherds and cattle herders. Today dogs of this striking breed are frequently seen in European countries. The breed is accepted and popular in the U.S.A. but still unknown in England.

Height approximately 26 in. at the shoulder, bitches slightly less. Colour pure white. Coat long on neck and croup but shorter and slightly wavy on sides. Tail reaching to below hocks and thickly covered in hair.

Labrador Retriever

In the early 19th century the water dogs—sometimes called St John's Dogs—from the eastern coast of Canada were in great demand by English shooting men. Many of these dogs were landed from the fishing vessels that worked the fishing grounds off Newfoundland and often berthed at Poole in Dorset. The passing of the quarantine laws was largely instrumental in stopping this easy method of importation. With stock already here, careful breeding produced the Labrador Retriever we know today, which is capable of working as a first class gundog, a police dog or simply being a charming companion. Recognised by the English Kennel Club in 1903, the Labrador Retriever is now known in every country of the world where a good shooting dog is appreciated.

Height approximately 22 in. Colour black, yellow or chocolate. Coat short and dense, free from wave and water resisting. Head rather broad with pronounced stop. Ears folding in close to the side; eyes brown or hazel. Tail thick, straight and tapering, resembling that of an otter.

Lakeland Terrier

Fell Terrier; Patterdale Terrier

   The title 'Lakeland Terrier' was one decided upon by the Lakeland Terrier Association about 1925, a few years before the Kennel Club gave the breed official recognition. Though these game little dogs had worked with almost all the hunts of their districts for many years, not until the formation of the Association in 1921 and the Lakeland Terrier Club in 1932 did the breed prosper as a Fancy. Today, however, the Lakeland is popular as a companion and Show dog.

   Height not to exceed $14\frac{1}{2}$ in. Weight not to exceed 17 lb. Colour blue and tan, blue, black, black and tan, red, wheaten or grizzle. Coat harsh, dense and weather-resisting. Head well balanced, flat skull, powerful jaws and broad but not overlong muzzle. Well set-on docked tail.

Lhasa Apso

The first Apsos to come to this country were brought from Tibet by returning members of the Younghusband Expedition in 1904, but it was the dogs imported by the Hon. Mrs Bailey in 1928 that really aroused interest. The term 'apso' is applied to any long-haired dog and derives from the resemblance of the hair to that of the native goats. They are gay and jaunty little dogs now to be seen at most of the major English and American shows.

Height 9–10 in. Coat is profuse, straight and hard with a heavy fall over the eyes and ample beard and whiskers. Colour: golden, sandy or honey preferred, but dark grizzle, slate, smoke or parti-colours of black, white or brown are permissible.

Löwchen Little Lion Dog

The Löwchen is not only a very old breed but it is a very rare one. These dogs have been known in Europe for some 500 years but there are only about fifty surviving today—four or five of them have recently come to England where it is hoped that they will thrive and multiply, the others being in Holland and Germany. Proof of the breed's antiquity is supplied by their appearance in several paintings including works by Marco Marziale and Goya. The Löwchen is a member of the Bichon family and should not be confused with the Asiatic breeds who are sometimes called Lion Dogs. In character Löwchen are gay, lively affectionate and intelligent. In appearance they are striking with coats clipped in the manner of a Miniature Poodle; the tail is left long with a lion-like tuft of hair at the tip.

Height approximately 10 in. Weight about 12 lb. Colour usually black, white, cream or grey.

Malinois Chien de Berger Belge

The Malinois, Laekenois and Tervueren are all
Belgian Shepherd Dogs from different areas and
varying only in their coats and colour.   The names
of the varieties are taken from the areas with which
they are mainly associated.   Nevertheless, Malinois and Tervueren have recently been accepted in
the United States.   All these dogs have the intelligence, courage, alertness and activity essential to a
shepherd dog and are excellent protectors of their
master and his property.

Height 24–26 in., bitches slightly less.   Head
and muzzle long and clean cut, ears erect.   Body
square with deep chest.   Legs strong and muscular.
Tail of medium length and carried low.   Coat:
Malinois—short, straight with dense undercoat;
Tervueren—long, well fitting straight and abundant; Laekenois—rough and wiry.   Colour: Malinois—rich fawn to mahogany with black overlay;
Tervueren—rich fawn to russet mahogany, black
tips to hair giving shaded effect, black mask and
ears; Laekenois—brown brindle.

Maltese

Without doubt the Maltese is the oldest of the
European Toy breeds, references having been
made to this race by Aristotle and Strabo as
coming from the island of Melita or Malta; later,
John Caius (1510–73) called the breed Melite.
As far back as 1763, when Sir Joshua Reynolds
painted the then leading beauty, Nellie O'Brien, he
showed her with a typical Maltese resting on her
lap. It came to England about the time of
Henry VIII, but was most popular in the 1880s.
During recent years this breed's charming appearance and endearing characteristics have done much
to increase its popularity.

Height not over 10 in. Head well balanced.
Eyes dark brown with black rims. Nose black.
Ears long and well feathered. Legs short and
straight. Body short and cobby. Coat pure
white, of good length and silky texture. Tail well
feathered and arched over back.

Manchester Terrier

Black and Tan Terrier

Purely British in its origin, and probably descended from the old broken-haired Black and Tan Terrier, the modern Manchester Terrier is best known in the North of England, and in Lancashire in particular. It had its heyday in the last half of the last century, when it was quite fashionable. With the ban on ear cropping becoming effective, the quality and popularity of the Manchester deteriorated, its specialist Club became defunct, and eventually the breed neared extinction. Recently, breeders have been able to repair the damage and there are a number of good dogs to be seen at the shows.

Height about 16 in., bitches about 15 in. Ears small and V-shaped, hanging close to the head. Colour jet black with rich mahogany tan markings. Coat close, smooth, short and glossy and of firm texture. Tail not docked.

97

Maremma Sheepdog

Abruzzi Sheepdog; Cane da Pastor Maremmano;
Maremmes Sheepdog

This breed, the more popular of the Italian
shepherd dogs, is common in Central Italy from
Tuscany to the Abruzzes, being used for herding
and guard work. The Maremma leads a hard life,
though often fed only on curds and whey. It is
recognised by the Italian Kennel Club as a pure
breed, and was imported into Britain first by
Mrs Home-Robertson in 1931, and now has several
devotees and a specialist club. However, it has
not gained the popularity it deserves and is not yet
known in the U.S.A.

Height 24–26 in. Weight about 70–75 lb.
(Pyrenean Mountain Dog massiveness should be
avoided.) Colour white, though sometimes lemon,
biscuit or fawn. Coat medium in length, soft,
lustrous and tight fitting. Head and body like the
Kuvasz but more refined; nose black; eyes opaque;
loins slightly arched; tail carried low.

Mastiff

Alan; Alaunt; Bandogge; Mollossus; Tie-dog

A wealth of history stands behind the Mastiff breed, dating back to centuries B.C. As a fighting dog it was used in most wars of Asia and Europe, by the Romans (who even had an officer titled the Procurator of Dogs stationed in Britain to send Mastiffs to the Roman Amphitheatres), and in the Middle Ages, in Britain, as a bear-baiting dog. It is certainly of Asiatic origin, coming to Britain through Epirus and the Phoenicians before the time of the Roman conquest. With the extinction of bear-baiting, the race went out of vogue, but recovered again. After the Second World War there was a risk of the breed becoming extinct in this country but the danger has been overcome.

Size, the larger the better, providing the dog is massive, powerful, symmetrical and sound. Colour apricot or silver fawn, dark fawn-brindle, always with black muzzle, ears and nose. Coat short, smooth and close-lying.

Miniature Pinscher

The term 'pinscher' approximates to 'terrier' and these small but game little dogs undoubtedly have many terrier characteristics. Dogs of this breed first came to England in 1938 but before they could become established, war broke out. In the U.S.A. Miniature Pinschers had gained a certain popularity some ten years earlier. In 1948 a determined and successful effort was made to popularise the breed in this country and stock was imported from the Continent and the U.S.A.

Height ranges from 10–12 in., preference being given to the smaller size. The coat is smooth, hard and short. Colours solid red or black, blue or chocolate with sharply defined tan markings. Ears small and either erect or dropped. Tail docked short and carried high.

Newfoundland

The Newfoundland is a relative of the St Bernard of Switzerland, but exactly how he came to be in Newfoundland is not known. The English and French were the first to import the breed back into Europe, and poets and painters have for centuries testified to its beauty and dignity. Bewick depicted the Newfoundland in 1790, whilst in his 'Twa Dogs' (1786), Rabbie Burns refers to the breed. The best known work is probably Landseer's painting of 1838, 'A Distinguished Member of the Humane Society', in the National Gallery of British Art. Newfoundlands are excellent water dogs and on several occasions they have saved the lives of humans and animals.

Height 28 in. Weight 150 lb. Colour usually dull black. Coat flat, medium length, rather coarse, slightly oily and capable of resisting water.

Norfolk Terrier

The early history of the Norfolk Terrier is identical with that of the Norwich Terrier (p. 104) and until 1964 the only difference in appearance was the carriage of the ears, and all were known as Norwich Terriers. After prolonged discussion amongst the breeders the Kennel Club gave its permission for the breed to divide. Those with erect ears remained Norwich Terriers whilst those with drop ears were given the breed title of Norfolk Terriers. It remains to be seen which breed will eventually become the most popular. These are independent, sporting and hardy little dogs, and the breed should have a bright future.

Height about 10 in. Colour red, red-wheaten, black and tan, or grizzle. Coat hard, wiry and straight. Skull fairly wide between the small, well carried, drop ears. Pointed 'foxy' muzzle.

Norwegian Buhund

In his native country the Norwegian Buhund is primarily a farm dog and is certainly akin to the Welsh Corgis. These dogs have all the attributes of the Spitz family with upstanding ears and a tail that curls over the back. This most intelligent breed appeared in England in 1946 and is supported by a large band of admirers. It achieved championship status in 1970. Not yet accepted in the U.S.A. Dogs exhibited in Britain are judged by the same standards as those in Norway where they are highly esteemed.

Height approx. 18 in. The double coat has long harsh top hair with a soft woolly undercoat, longer on the neck and body than the head and limbs. The skull is lean, light and wedge-shaped, being broadest between the ears.

Norwich Terrier

The dates 1870 and 1880 are those most often quoted when referring to the origin of the Norwich Terrier, but dogs of this type existed long before then, although not called by their present name. The breed is descended from some small Irish Terriers used in Norfolk for fox and badger working, probably crossed with other British hunting Terriers, and bred to a size not exceeding 12 in. Not widely known, the Norwich was not recognised in Britain until 1932, when the breed Club was formed, and neither was it accepted as a pure breed in America until 1936, when the American Kennel Club gave it official status. It is a gay and friendly little dog, deserving popularity.

Height 10–11 in. Weight 11–13 lb. Colour red, black and tan, wheaten or grizzle. Coat as hard and wiry as possible, quite straight, and close-lying. Ears erect. Tail docked.

Old English Sheepdog

Bobtail Sheepdog

The Old English Sheepdog is an ancient breed of great charm and sagacity. Although now seldom used as a working sheepdog, the 'Bobtail' makes an excellent guard and caretaker. These dogs enjoy looking after their master's property whether it be the house, children or chickens. Bobtails are strongly and compactly built but of great symmetry. The heavy coat and characteristic ambling or pacing movement at the walk is apt to give an erroneous impression of slowness and clumsiness, whereas these dogs are, in fact, very active. Some puppies of the breed are born tailless but docking is usually necessary.

Height about 22 in. Colour grey, grizzle, blue or blue-merle, with or without white markings. The coat is shaggy and of hard texture with a weather-resisting undercoat, and is particularly abundant on hind-quarters and head.

Otterhound

For many centuries the otter has been hunted in England; the earliest references are those made to the Hounds of King John and other 13th-century packs. These were not the Otterhounds of the type seen today, being then very promiscuously bred and much slower in action. The modern Otterhound is the product of the Southern Hound, Bloodhound, Griffon Vendéen and the Welsh Hound. The tendency today is, unfortunately, to use mixed packs of Otterhounds and Foxhounds, and crosses of the two breeds, rather than maintain the pure race, which is infinitely superior. The Otterhound has been recognised by the American Kennel Club since 1907 and used in the U.S.A. for general sport.

Height 24 in. Weight 65 lb. Colour grizzle, black, blue or red, with tan markings. Coat hard, crisp and not too long, with woolly undercoat.

Papillon

Phalènes

Little dogs of this type must have long been popular pets at many European courts since they appear in so many paintings by Italian, Florentine, Flemish, Dutch, French and English artists.

The breed gained its name from its large, heavily fringed and upstanding ears that are set obliquely on a rounded skull with a narrow white blaze. The resemblance to a butterfly is very striking. Another variety of the breed have drop ears and are known as Phalènes.

Height 8–11 in. Weight $3\frac{1}{2}$–7 lb. Coat long, fine and silky. Colour white with patches that may be of any colour except liver. The tail well fringed and curved up and over the back.

Pekingese

Pekingese were introduced in 1860, when, after the sacking of the Summer Palace in Peking, three Allied officers brought back five of the Imperial pets. One of these, 'Looty', was presented to Queen Victoria. After the death of the Empress Tzu Hsi, in 1911, the fine Palace specimens became rare, and the breed has generally fallen into neglect in China. Most of the good Pekingese in Britain and America are descendants of stock smuggled out of China at the end of the last century. The breed is very popular.

Weight 7–12 lb. With the exception of liver all colours, including white, are permissible. Particolours should be evenly broken. Coat long, straight and flat, with profuse feathering on thighs, legs, toes and tail. Head wide and flat between the ears, with short wrinkled muzzle; body leonine; tail curled and plumed.

Pharaoh Hound

The likeness between the hounds that have recently come to England from Malta and the hounds depicted by the Egyptians 5000 years ago is remarkable. Those assiduous traders, the Phoenicians, probably took hounds from Egypt with them on their ships as they travelled around the shores of the Mediterranean. Little colonies of hounds on Malta and the nearby island of Gozo seem to have remained very cut off from outside influences through the centuries. Since the farmers and peasants have taken an interest in the breeding of the hounds that are so useful to them for hunting rabbits their appearance has changed remarkably little over the years. Their ancient lineage has given these graceful hounds great dignity although they are friendly and playful.

Height approx. 22 in. Head long, lean and well chiselled with flesh-coloured nose, amber eyes and moderately large erect ears. Coat short and smooth. Colour always tan with white on chest, toes, and tip of whip-like tail which is carried over the back.

Pointer

Like the Spaniel group, the Pointer originated in Spain, where, during the early 17th century, it was famous for its ability to point to the bird with its nose, body and tail in a straight line. At that time, it was a slow and ponderous animal. In an attempt to produce a speedier dog a cross of Foxhound blood was introduced at the time but without success since the hound's instinct is to seek scent on the ground whilst a setting dog should find it in the air. The Pointer was one of the two breeds at the first British dog show held at Newcastle in 1859.

Height 24½ in. Weight 50–55 lb. Colour white with liver, black or lemon markings although whole blacks are sometimes seen. Coat short and smooth. Ears long, thin and silky; body lithe and muscular; the deep muzzle should be somewhat concave; tail long and tapering; should lash from side to side when the dog is moving.

Pomeranian

Being a miniature Spitz, the Pomeranian has a close affinity with the Arctic breeds, such as the Samoyed, Elkhound and Finnish Spitz, the Central European Keeshond and the Italian Volpino. When first introduced into Britain, it was almost like the German Wolfspitz of today, but gradually became smaller, until the old 20–30 lb dog disappeared and the modern Toy took its place. In the early days the breed did not attract much attention, but with Queen Victoria patronising the fancy in 1888 and the formation of the first breed club in 1891, the Pomeranian became popular.

Weight about 5 lb, but often as little as 3–4 lb. Colour red, orange, orange-sable, wolf-sable, beaver, blue, white, brown, chocolate and black. Coat long, straight, profuse and offstanding around the neck and shoulders.

Poodle (Standard)

Pudel

France, Germany and Russia have all claimed the Poodle. Poodles were certainly known in Italy in the 16th century and in Holland in the 17th century; they did not arrive in this country until considerably later. On the Continent the Poodle was frequently used as a water spaniel, hence its name which derives from the German 'puddeln', to splash in water. Recently the larger and original members of this intelligent family have been less favoured than their smaller parvenu brethren but there are signs that their popularity is increasing.

Height 15 in. and over. Colour black, white, brown, blue or any solid colour. The profuse, offstanding coat is of hard texture and is usually clipped in the traditional 'lion' style.

Poodle (Miniature)

Small Poodles, almost always white or parti-coloured, can be seen in many 17th- and 18th-century paintings and were certainly fashionable pets at that period but it seems likely that these were the result of a cross with a Maltese or other small breed. It was in the early years of the 20th century that systematic and ultimately successful attempts were made to breed small, typical pure-bred Poodles and in 1911 the English Kennel Club acknowledged them as a separate breed. It was not until the end of the Second World War that the breed really captured the fancy of dog lovers both here and in the U.S.A.—since when their popularity has been phenomenal.

Height under 15 in. In all other respects the Miniature Poodle is a replica of the Standard Poodle.

Poodle (Toy)

A very small dog has great charm for many people. With the Miniature Poodle enjoying such tremendous popularity on both sides of the Atlantic, American breeders and admirers of these little dogs began to breed them yet smaller and it was not long before British breeders followed suit. The earliest attempts were not very successful but within a few years very tiny and quite typical Poodles were being bred and in the 1950s the Toy Poodle became a third and officially accepted member of the family.

Height must be under 11 in. In the U.S.A. under 10 in. In all other respects the standard is the same as for the two larger varieties.

Portuguese Podengo

Portuguese Rabbit Dog; Portuguese Warren
Hound

Of the nine native breeds of dogs of Portugal
the most common is the Podengo, seen all over
the country and used almost exclusively for rabbit
hunting. The breed is divided into three sizes,
the Grande or large, Médio or medium-sized, and
the Pequeño or small variety; the Grande and
Pequeño Podengos are well distributed throughout
Portugal, being favourites in town and country.
Two have recently been imported into England.

Heights (Grande) 22–27 in., (Médio) 16–20 in.,
(Pequeño) 12–16 in. Colour any fawn or yellow
shade, from cream to deep chestnut or faded black,
but not grey. May be whole coloured with or
without white markings. Coat short, smooth and
dense. Ears erect. Head foxy. Tail strong and
thick, set on high.

Pug

Carlin; Mops

The Pug, like so many short-nosed breeds, originated in China. By the 16th century Pugs were known in Europe and were especially favoured in the Netherlands. When William and Mary came to the English throne their Pugs came with them and displaced the small spaniels who had previously been the court favourites. At the end of the last century Pugs were in great favour and when Lady Brassey exhibited her black Pugs there was a considerable sensation. In the following years the Pomeranian and the Pekingese were amongst the favoured 'toy' breeds but now Pugs have regained their world-wide popularity.

Weight 14–18 lb. Colours silver-fawn, apricot-fawn or black. With the first two the ears and mask should be as black as possible. Coat fine, smooth, short and glossy. Muzzle short and square. Tail curled tightly over hip.

Puli

The Puli (plural Pulik) has worked for the Hungarian shepherds for the past 1000 years. The coat of the Puli is remarkable—the undercoat soft, woolly and very dense, the outercoat long and profuse. Since a working dog is seldom groomed, thick mats are formed and protect the dog in the bitter weather and biting winds when he will seldom have a roof over his head. The more domesticated dogs seen in the cities of eastern Europe, sometimes in America and occasionally in England are usually well brushed and the coat hangs in luxuriant strands.

Height approximately 17 in. An extremely active dog with the characteristic coat which may be black, white, rusty black or various shades of grey. Ears V-shaped and hanging. Tail sometimes a natural bob, otherwise long, carried over back when alert or low with the end curled when at rest.

Pyrenean Mountain Dog Great Pyrenees

These large, powerful and very sagacious dogs
are akin to the Kuvasz, Maremma Sheepdogs and
all herding breeds whose ancestors arrived in Europe
with the Aryan migration. In 1675 the young
Dauphin returned to the Louvre from a visit to
Barrège accompanied by a 'patou' or Mountain dog
and the breed became fashionable at Court.
Nevertheless, the basic work for the majority of
these dogs was the guarding of the flocks and herds
in the lonely mountain pastures where wolves and
wild animals were common, their only protection,
apart from their thick coats, being a wide iron spiked
collar. The breed became somewhat neglected
until the present century when it became very
popular first in Britain and, later, in the U.S.A.

Height 27–32 in. Weight 100–125 lb. Colour
all white or principally white with markings of
badger, grey or tan. Coat very resistant to weather;
thick outer coat of coarse hair and undercoat of
finer hair. Always double dew claws on back feet.

Rhodesian Ridgeback

Rhodesian Lion Dog

The most generally accepted view is that this breed is the product of the Bloodhound and the Hottentot Hunting Dog, the latter supplying the characteristic ridge of hair which grows in the opposite direction to the rest of the coat. The work for which they were originally intended was the tracking and bringing to bay of lions. It was essential that they should be strong and fearless.

Height 25–27 in., bitches 24–26 in. Weight 85 lb, bitches 75 lb. Colour light to red wheaten. Coat short and dense, sleek and glossy, but neither woolly nor silky. The ridge should start immediately behind the shoulders and continue to the hip bones, and should contain two identical crowns opposite each other. The lower edges of the crowns should not extend further than one-third of the length of the ridge.

Rottweiler

Named after the town of Rottweil, the Rottweiler is a well-known cattle dog on the Continent. Centuries ago it was used by the Swabian knights in the chase of the wild boar with some similar breeds which are now extinct. As a drovers' dog, the Rottweiler excels, and recently it has been developed and trained as guide-dog, police tracker and army dog. The breed is established in the U.S.A. and there is an increasing amount of interest in this country. The first English Champion was made up in 1966.

Height 23–27 in. Colour black, with well-defined mahogany or tan markings. Coat of medium length, coarse and flat with undercoat. Head rather broad with good stop; ears pendant; body muscular; tail docked very short.

St Bernard

Alpine Mastiff

The St Bernard is a noble breed very widely known but his size prevents his becoming more popular than he is. As rescuers of lost wayfarers in the Swiss Alps, the dogs of St Bernard Hospice were world famous, their deeds being prodigious. 'Barry', a dog now mounted in the Berne Museum, saved forty lives before losing his own! The breed came to England about 1810. The St Bernard Club of America was founded in 1888 and is one of the oldest specialist clubs in the U.S.A.

Height, the taller the better, providing symmetry is maintained. Colour orange, mahogany-brindle, red-brindle or white with patches of these colours. The coat can be rough or smooth.

Saluki

Gazelle Hound; Persian Greyhound

The Saluki is one of the oldest branches of the greyhound family tree and can trace its history for at least 5000 years. Until recently the breeding of these hounds has been mainly in the hands of the Arab sheiks who esteemed them highly and used them for working with falcons and gazelle hunting. The Hon. Florence Amherst began to import Salukis into England in 1897 and they are now amongst the most popular of the hound breeds, but it was not recognised in the U.S.A. until 1927. A dignified, graceful and faithful breed.

Height 23–28 in., bitches 20–25. Colours white, cream, golden, red-fawn, black and tan, grizzle or tricolour. Coat smooth, soft and silky, long on the ears, legs and tail.

Samoyed

Samojedskaja

One of the most beautiful members of the Spitz family, the Samoyed is named after the nomadic tribe of Samoyeds, or Samoyedes, usually found at the head of the Yenisei, though the dogs are common to the Pechora district and even further afield. The general title of Laiki is given to some half-dozen of these Northern breeds, which are used for rounding up reindeer, guarding the herds, and sometimes as sled dogs. The earliest importation of any note was a dog brought by Mr Kilburn Scott in 1889, which was followed by others within a few years. Sometimes called 'the smiling dog'. The Samoyed Club was founded in 1909, and since then the breed has forged ahead.

Height 20–22 in. Weight about 45–55 lb. Colour white, white and biscuit, and cream. Coat harsh, medium to long, with a stand-off ruff, and thick soft undercoat.

Schipperke

Belgian Barge Dog

The Schipperke ('Little Skipper') is a well-known breed in the Netherlands, and particularly in the Louvain district. It was once used for guarding barges and river boats, although it served a multitude of other purposes as well. Perky and adaptable, with an inbred affection for canals and tow-horses, the Schipperke is becoming popular generally. It was not until 1885, when the Queen of the Belgians became interested in it, that it made any substantial headway. However, in 1887 it was imported into England and by 1890 the English Schipperke Club had been formed.

Height 12–13 in. Weight 12–16 lb. Colour jet black but other whole colours permissible. Coat harsh, short and smooth on the head, ears and leg, but frilled round the neck. Head foxy; ears small, erect; body muscular; tail docked very close.

Schnauzer

Although this breed, with its three varieties of size, is squarely built like the Terrier family, it has never been actually called by the name of Schnauzer Terrier. It is principally a general purpose dog used in Germany, Austria and Switzerland as a drovers' dog, watch-dog, police-dog and companion. A statue of the Night-watchman and his Dog, in Stuttgart, dated 1620, shows a typical Schnauzer of medium size, whilst paintings of a century earlier depict the breed as of quite a well-defined type. The large-sized variety is still rare in England, but the Standard and Miniature are well established. The Duchess of Montrose was the pioneer of the breed in Britain when about 40 years ago it was first introduced. The Schnauzer Club of America was formed in 1925.

Height 18–19 in. Colour all pepper and salt colours or pure black. Coat hard and wiry with whiskers on muzzle.

Schnauzer (Miniature)

Zwergschnauzer

The Miniature Schnauzer should be a perfect, reduced copy of the Standard or Medium Schnauzer in design, usefulness and character. About 50 years ago, small editions of the Schnauzer were being exhibited in Germany, but the Miniature did not arrive in England until about 1928, when some fine stock was flown over for Mr W. H. Hancock, who became the pioneer and founder of most of the British stock. Miniatures had already, in about 1923, been introduced into America, where today the variety is quite fashionable.

Height 14 in., bitches not over 13 in. Colour all pepper and salt colours or pure black. (*See* Schnauzer.)

Scottish Terrier

Aberdeen Terrier

The National Terrier of Scotland is an ancient race descended from an old broken-haired Terrier of the Highlands used centuries ago for sporting purposes, with possibly a little Skye and Yorkshire Terrier blood added. The title Scottish Terrier was used in the general sense for any of the Scottish Cairns, West Highland Whites, Skyes and even Dandie Dinmonts until this century. Today the Scottish Terrier is one of the most popular of the terrier breeds and his loyal and determined nature makes him an outstanding companion.

Height about 10–11 in. Weight 19–23 lb. Colour jet black (the most fashionable), brindle and wheaten. Coat wiry and medium length. Head fairly long; ears small and erect; back short; tail thick at set-on, tapering and gay.

Sealyham Terrier

Of all the breeds to come from the Welsh Principality the Sealyham is generally the most popular. Although not created until the year 1851, when Capt. John Tucker-Edwardes of Sealyham (a village near Haverfordwest) designed the breed especially for badger-baiting, the Sealyham has forged ahead of many other breeds of older history. At Haverfordwest, Pembrokeshire, the first Sealyhams were shown, but the large arenas of the Kennel Club event of 1910 were really the starting point for the breed. Though now usually bred for companionship, the Sealyham is a very useful sporting terrier when required. In the U.S.A. the Sealyham Terrier is tremendously popular.

Height 10–12 in. Weight 18–20 lb. Colour white entirely or with lemon, brown or badger pied markings on head and ears. Coat long, hard and wiry.

Shetland Sheepdog

Peerie Dog; Toonie Dog

The Shetland Islands are the home of diminutive ponies and sheep and it is understandable that the latter should be taken charge of by diminutive sheepdogs with a strong resemblance to a small-sized Collie. In the Zetland dialect these were known as 'peerie' or fairy dogs. Collie breeders were strongly against the breed becoming known as Shetland Collies and after discussion the breed title of Shetland Sheepdog was accepted in 1914. The breed's charm has won it many admirers on both sides of the Atlantic.

Height 14 in. Colours black and tan with white, black with white, sable, sable with white, black with tan, blue-merle and blue-merle with white. Outer coat long, harsh and straight with soft undercoat. Definite mane. Ears semi-erect when alert. Tail long with abundant hair.

Shih Tzu

The Shih Tzu (pronounced *sheedzoo*) is small in stature but remarkable for courage, charming personality and an almost comical arrogance of bearing. Shih Tzus descend from the Apsos of Tibet which were often presented as tributes to the Emperors of China. The Chinese had a fondness for short-faced dogs and over the course of the years the Shih Tzu developed a rounded skull, square and broad muzzle with a nose of about an inch in length. The Chinese were reluctant to part with their best dogs but in 1930 the late Sir Douglas and Lady Brownrigg and Miss Hutchins brought some carefully selected dogs to England. Progress was slow, but the breed is now established in Europe and was admitted to the A.K.C. register in 1969.

Weight 9–16 lb. Never higher than 10½ in. at withers. All colours, but a white blaze on forehead and tip of tail is highly prized. Coat long and dense; profuse hair on head falls over eyes. Tail plumed and curled over back.

Skye Terrier

Like the Scottish breeds the Skye Terrier is an old race, which was used at least three centuries ago for earth work, its long low-to-ground body being admirably designed for badger pipes and fox bolts. Early references to the breed described it as a 'Cur brought out of barbarous borders', but this once-seen-never-forgotten breed is today by no means a low-bred dog, except in size! For over 30 years Queen Victoria maintained a keen interest in the Skye, and it was doubtless through her instrumentality that the breed came into the public eye. Lately, since the breed has become less a Terrier and more a fancier's dog it has become larger and longer and great emphasis is placed on length of coat. The Skye Terrier is an alert and vigorous watch-dog.

Height about 10 in. Weight 24–30 lb. Length from nose to tail tip about 41½ in. Colour blue-grey, fawn and cream with black points. Coat long, hard, flat. Ears prick or drop.

Soft-coated Wheaten Terrier

Irish Wheaten Terrier

The exact origin of this Irish breed is not known, but wheaten-coloured Terriers of soft coats have existed in Ireland for a considerable time. Certainly the type of this little known breed has not changed for at least 80 years, and, being fixed by the Standard of Points now drawn up by the breed Club, will remain unchanged. In Eire no dog can qualify for championship honours without a working certificate. In England the breed has a small but staunch band of supporters. These dogs are loyal and sporting terriers, unspoilt in any way.

Height about 17 in. Weight 35 lb, bitches 32 lb. Colour good clear wheaten; a few white hairs on the chest penalise, but do not disqualify. Coat abundant and soft, wavy or with large loose curls.

Staffordshire Bull Terrier

The Staffordshire Bull Terrier was seldom seen in the south of England until the early 1920s and it was not until the 1930s that the breed was officially recognised by the English Kennel Club. In the U.S.A. the breed has been known since about 1870 and American dogs are somewhat heavier than those favoured in England. The Staffordshire of both countries is strong, brave and intelligent.

Height 14–16 in. Weight 28–38 lb. Colour any brindle, black, blue, red, fawn and white, or any of these with white. Coat short, smooth and close.

Sussex Spaniel

This English gundog is named after the county of Sussex, where, at the end of the 18th century, it was first bred. The pioneer of the breed was Mr Fuller of Rosehill Park, near Hastings, who, by the time of his death in 1847, had bred Sussex Spaniels for half a century. His dogs were the ancestors of most of the present-day specimens. The Sussex is a slow worker but intensely conscientious, while it differs from most sporting dogs by giving tongue when on the scent. It is this habit of babbling that has made it rather unpopular with present-day shooting men. It is a low-to-ground dog purposely bred so in order to push through and under brambles and thickets rather than clamber over them like a Springer.

Height 16 in., bitches 15 in. Weight about 45 lb. Colour rich golden liver. Coat short, abundant, flat, with moderate featherings on legs and stern.

Swiss Mountain Dog

Grosse Schweizer Sennenhund; Large Swiss
Mountain Dog

For the sake of clarity the above title is intended
in this work to refer only to the largest of the
Sennenhund: the Appenzell, Bernese and Entlebuch Mountain Dogs have their specific breed
nomenclature, while this largest type has not;
hence the use of the general title in a specific
instance. It is the most widely used of Swiss
draught dogs, seen in almost all Cantons hauling
waggons laden with cheeses, cans of milk, loaves
of bread, and other produce. The dogs are
scrupulously cared for and protected by laws
governing designs of harness, weights of loads and
measurements of the dog's height. Licences are
issued only after the strictest investigation of the
dog, cart and owner.

Height 26–31 in. Weight 75–100 lb. Colour
the attractive tricolour of jet black, deep russet
brown and white. Coat short and close-fitting.

Sydney Silky

Silky Terrier

Very much like the Australian Terrier, this breed originated about the environs of Sydney, Australia. It is descended from the Australian and Yorkshire Terriers, though it is likely that the Skye Terrier also played a small part in the early days. The breed is regarded as quite distinct in Australasia, and is recognised as such both there and in the U.S.A., where it is increasing in popularity. It first attracted attention in Britain about 1930, when a few were exhibited. It is a game and inquisitive little fellow, with much of the inherited intelligence of the Yorkshire Terrier.

Height 9–10 in. Weight 8–10 lb. Colour blue and tan, often with dark mask. Profuse hair on top of head forms a top-knot. Coat silken in texture and about 6 in. long. Tail is docked close and carried erect.

Tibetan Spaniel

Tibetan Prayer Dog

Something like a Pekingese with short hair on the back and flanks, the Tibetan Spaniel is quaintly attractive. In Tibet it has been highly prized for many centuries and was usually bred in the monasteries and valued for its watchfulness. Classified as a non-sporting breed, the smaller specimens are the most valued and hardest to obtain. The breed is well known in India and has become popular in Britain, but is not recognised in the U.S.A.

Height about 11 in. Weight 9–16 lb. Colour golden, cream, white, biscuit, fawn, sable, black, parti-colours or tricolour. Coat silky with ample feathering. Ears pendant; tail curled over the back.

Tibetan Terrier

Darjeeling Terrier

This old Tibetan breed has an interesting history. The breed is well known in India, but is now attracting notice in England, where it appears at most of the major shows. These dogs are alert, intelligent and sporting, but are not true terriers, often being used for herding in their native land. Not yet accepted in the U.S.A.

Height 14–15 in. Weight 14–30 lb. Colour white, cream, grey, golden, parti-colour and black. Coat long, profuse and fine, without being silky or curly. Head rather broad, of medium length; ears pendant, close and feathered; body compact and straight backed; legs straight and well boned; tail medium length, well plumed and carried gaily.

Vallhund

Västgöta Spets

This Swedish herding dog is probably of ancient
descent. It has been used for centuries as a drover
of cattle in Sweden, and although once nearly
extinct has lately been revived. The best specimens have been found in Västgötland and Halland,
neighbouring cattle-rearing provinces in south-
west Sweden, where today breeding from selected
dogs is taking place. Officially recognised in 1942,
it is now attracting attention in Scandinavia. The
Vallhund and the Welsh Corgi are distantly related.
The breed is rarely seen in this country.

Height 12–15 in. Weight 20–30 lb. Colour
usually grey with dark mask, ears and saddle,
though some are light red. Coat short and hard
with thick, soft undercoat. Ears erect and sharp-
pointed. Tail generally a mere stump.

Vizsla

Hungarian Pointer; Yellow Pointer

Of the ten national breeds of dogs of Hungary, the Vizsla is the sole shooting dog, a breed which combines the duties of Pointer, Setter and Retriever. It is admirably suited to the game and conditions of the puszta. The Vizsla is expected to work fast, first finding his game by scent, then pointing and, after it is shot, retrieving it. The breed is attracting attention in this country at the present time and appears to have a bright future.

Height 25 in. Weight 70–75 lb. Colour dark sandy yellow. The coat is short and dense and without undercoat. Tail docked by about one-third.

Weimaraner

The Weimaraner is well established in Great Britain where it made its first appearance about 1953. Much of the original stock was imported from the U.S.A. where the breed had aroused interest as early as 1929. It originated as a sporting dog at the Court of Weimar in the 19th century. Almost certainly there is a link between the Weimaraner and the German Short-haired Pointer but the Weimaraner is remarkable for its silver or mouse-grey colouring and light amber eyes. An intelligent and friendly breed and a good worker with the gun.

Height 22–25 in. Weight 45–65 lb. Coat usually short, smooth and sleek. Long-coated specimens sometimes seen. Ears long and lobular and set on high. Tail docked to about 6 in.

Welsh Corgi (Cardiganshire)

Separate classification for the two varieties of the Welsh Corgi were allotted by the English Kennel Club in 1934, and since then the Cardiganshire type has been seen on its own in Show classes. The fillip given to the Pembrokeshire variety by Royal patronage has left the Cardigan dog rather behind in popularity, but in its native county it is still a cattle-dog par excellence, and extremely valuable to the Welsh farmers.

Height 12 in. Weight 22–26 lb. Colour any colour except pure white. Coat short or medium and of hard texture; upstanding ears rather large in proportion to head. Tail moderately long and carried in line with body. (*See* Welsh Corgi, Pembrokeshire.)

Welsh Corgi (Pembrokeshire)

Ci Sawdl; Welsh Heeler

The origin of this Welsh cattle-dog is lost in antiquity; it seems to be the cattle-dog referred to in the old laws of Wales codified by King Hywel Dda in 920. For many centuries, the drovers' dog was the only breed known in Wales. Today, the Corgi is known the world over, and it has also become immensely popular in America. With the modern tendency towards small houses and flats, the Corgi has become well established as a house dog and companion in the town as well as the countryside. (*See* Vallhund.)

Height preferably 10–12 in. Weight 20–24 lb. Colour self red, sable, fawn, black and tan or with white markings on head, legs, chest and neck. Coat medium length, smooth and dense. Ears comparatively large and erect; tail short or absent.

Welsh Hound

Bytheuad; Welsh Foxhound

The mountainous country of Wales has determined the design of her native hunting dogs, and so the Welsh Hound is a low-scenting dog, stouthearted, with good shoulders, and talkative. (Generous voice is needed in the winding defiles of Welsh hunting country.) It is an ancient race, probably descended from the extinct Celtic Hound and the old Staghound. Celebrated packs of pure Welsh Hounds were kept nearly 200 years ago, while names like Llangibby, Neuadd-Fawr, Ynysfor and Gelligaer will remain among the front rank of Welsh hunting.

Height 24 in. Weight about 70–75 lb. Colour black and fawn, red, tan, lemon and mixed. Coat rough, medium length, dense or smooth and short.

Welsh Springer Spaniel

Red and White Spaniel; Starter; Tarfgi

The Springer Spaniel of Wales is slightly smaller than its English cousin and is easily recognised by its red and white colouring. In Wales it is often called the Tarfgi or 'dispersing-dog', being very popular there, where it is used for water work as well as on land. It is probably descended from the Spaniels referred to in the Ancient Laws of Wales, codified in the 10th century. An active and high-spirited dog, the Welsh Springer Spaniel was officially recognised in 1902. After the last war it became rare but has now gained ground and is often seen at shows and as a companion in Britain, the U.S.A. and most dog-loving countries.

Weight 35–45 lb. Dogs not to exceed 19 in. at shoulder, bitches 18 in. Colour dark, rich red and white. Coat straight, thick and of silky texture. Ears set low, fairly small and vine-leaf shaped. Tail, ears and legs lightly feathered.

Welsh Terrier

It is known that pedigree Welsh Terriers existed in 1854, and the the breed had its first show classes at Pwllheli, about 1885. At their first public appearances these dogs were entered in classes for 'Welsh or Old English Wire-haired Black and Tan Terriers.' There was considerable discussion before the title 'Welsh Terrier' was adopted. It is *not* a large-sized Lakeland, and neither should it be a miniature Airedale, though to the uninitiated its pattern is not dissimilar to either of these tan and black-saddled Terriers. The breed is a very sporting one and the dogs make active and intelligent companions greatly valued in most dog-loving countries.

Height about 15 in. Weight about 20 lb. Colour black and tan or black-grizzle and tan. Coat hard and very close and wiry.

West Highland White Terrier

Poltalloch Terrier; Roseneath Terrier

Here is the only all-white Scottish breed and a native of Argyll, if one part of Scotland has more claim than any other. The great pioneer of the breed was Colonel Malcolm, of Poltalloch, who took great pains to establish just the right type for working the difficult terrain of the Western Highlands. For many years white puppies appeared in the litters of Cairn Terriers and the two varieties were frequently inter-bred. Owing to objections from the U.S.A. this ceased after 1925. The breed holds its own in numerical strength and reputation in the United Kingdom and the U.S.A.

Height 11 in. Weight 15–18 lb. Colour white. Coat about 2 in. long, hard and free from curl, with a short, soft and close undercoat. Ears small, triangular and erect or semi-erect. Body well muscled with a relatively strong thick tail.

Whippet

The Whippet's ancestors were probably Greyhounds, Manchester Terriers and English White
Terriers. Racing was popularised by Freeman
Lloyd, the Welsh sporting writer, who with Sir
John Astley introduced Edward VII to the sport in
1894. The dog resembles a typical Greyhound in
miniature, and was officially recognised by the
English Kennel Club in 1895. Whippets are now
one of the universally popular breeds since their
close coats give no trouble and the dogs are
affectionate, intelligent and seldom aggressive.

Height $18\frac{1}{2}$ in., bitches $17\frac{1}{2}$ in. Weight 21 lb,
bitches 20 lb. Any colour or mixture of colours.
Coat fine, short and close. Ears rose-shaped and
small and fine in texture.

Yorkshire Terrier

The diminutive Terrier of Yorkshire is purely an English product, which was evolved about a century ago by artisans of the West Riding. Exactly what ingredients were used is not known, but the Scottish, Old English Broken-haired, Clydesdale and other small Terriers probably had a big say in its make-up. In fact, until about 1870 the breed was often classified as Broken-haired Scottish Terriers. Originally the Yorkshire Terrier was about 12–15 lb in weight, quite game, and a hardy varmint, but today it is about half that weight, longer and silkier coated, and not so much the ratter and earth-dog but, nevertheless, very game. The Yorkshire Terrier is the most popular toy breed in England at present.

Height 7–8 in. Weight up to 7 lb. Colour dark steel-blue and tan, the tan being dark at the roots, paling off to a light shade at the tips. Great importance is given to the straight and silky texture of the coat and its colour and length.

Descriptions of Less Familiar Breeds

Abyssinian Sand Terrier (African Hairless Dog) Related to the other hairless breeds. Their place of origin and the reason for their hairlessness has never been satisfactorily explained. The sandy-coloured or mottled Abyssinian Sand Terrier differs from other hairless varieties in that its ears are 'rose' or backward lying, while the others are erect.

Alano Mentioned as early as the 16th century and at one time used in Spain for bull baiting. Today these powerful dogs are used in packs for hunting wild boar. Nevertheless, they are of Mastiff descent and akin to the Dogue de Bordeaux (p. 154).

Arkwright Pointer (Black Pointer) This is not a separate breed but refers to a celebrated strain of Pointers owned and bred by Mr William Arkwright in the late 19th century, some of which were black.

Australian Cattle Dog (Australian Heeler) This is a breed manufactured in Australia and includes the blood of the Dingo as well as Collies, Kelpies and, probably, Dalmatians. These dogs which work silently are used exclusively for cattle droving and have proved their value on the cattle stations. They appear on the Australian show bench. Height 19–20 in. Weight 32–35 lb. Coat short, harsh and straight, blue-merle in colour or sometimes red or blue speckled.

Aztec Sacred Dog (Teechichi)   A small Pug-like dog said to have been worshipped by the Aztecs and taken by them to Mexico.   Possibly part-ancestor of the Chihuahua.

Baganda Hunting Dog   These native African hunting dogs are usually worked in packs to beat elephant grass and scrub for deer, gazelle, buffalo and even elephants.   Short-haired, high on the leg, prick-eared and with a ring tail, these dogs stand about 19½ in.   Colour fawn, tan or black and white.

Beauceron (Berger de Beauce)   A large, short-coated French herding breed with cropped ears and a long tail.   These dogs are active and muscular, standing between 23½ and 27½ in.   The short, close-lying coat is usually black, black and tan, red, grey or grey with black markings.

Bergamaschi (Cane da Pastor Bergamasco; Italian Bergama Sheepdog)   Next to the Maremma Sheepdog, this breed is the most popular working shepherd dog in Italy.   Like its cousin, it is an offshoot of the Kuvasz, with probably a little added Komondor blood.   Named after the Bergamo, Lombardy, region, the Bergamasco is recognised by the Italian Kennel Club and exhibited from time to time at shows.   It is not very well known outside Italy, although as a type it merits interest.

Height about 24 in.   Colour all white, fawn or grey.   Coat profuse, medium to long, often un-dulating or matted on the hind-quarters, where it is longest.   Muzzle often bearded; body rugged and square; tail long.

Bichon A generic name for a family of small Continental dogs which are usually long coated. It includes the Maltese, Havanese, Bolognese, Tenerife Dog and the Löwchen. The Maltese (p. 96) is the only breed of the family with a standard accepted by the English Kennel Club and American Kennel Club.

Blue Paul An extinct type once found in Western Scotland and valued for its fighting ability.

Border Collie Although not accepted for show purposes the Border Collie is a frequent competitor at the Sheepdog Trials and Obedience Competitions as well as being a practical working breed. Height $17\frac{1}{2}$–$19\frac{1}{2}$ in. Weight 42–52 lb. Coat of medium length and slightly wavy. Colour usually black or black and white. Tail with white tip.

Bouvier des Ardennes (Ardennes Cattle Dog) This is an old Belgian breed of droving dog that is also valued as a watch dog and companion. A muscular dog with a rough coat and generally tailless. Erect ears are preferred but coat colour immaterial.

Braque du Bourbonnais This is a descendant from the old French Braque, inheriting that breed's adaptability and aptitude for all-purpose work with game. Said to have a history going back 500 years. The coat is short, dense and inclined to be oily. The tail is docked very short and the ears are large and triangular. Colour white with chestnut or red-fawn flecks evenly distributed over body. Height about 22 in.

Braque St Germain This breed was created in the reign of Charles X from the mating of an orange and white Pointer bitch named 'Miss' with an old type of orange and white French Braque. Height 21–24 in. Coat short and soft. Colour white with bright orange spots or patches.

Canaan Dog A recently domesticated branch of the Pariah family and now officially accepted by the Israel and British Kennel Clubs. The standard requires a medium-sized short-haired dog with some resemblance to a Collie. Height $19\frac{1}{2}$–$23\frac{1}{2}$ in. Weight 40–55 lb. Coat usually short or medium length and thick; sandy, reddish brown, white or black in colour, with white markings permissible. Prick ears desirable as are bushy tails carried high.

Catalan Herder These dogs are descended from the old breed of Spanish Mastiff. Two types are accepted—the larger and long-coated Gos d'Atura which may be of several colours or the smaller, shorter-coated Gos d'Atura Cerda. These are by descent hardy cattle dogs but are often used as guards and companions.

Chien Fauve de Bretagne (Brittany Hound) This breed was originally introduced into Brittany in the 5th century by Welsh colonists who may have crossed them with the ancestors of the Breton Bassets. Originally it was a 24–25 in. hound used for wolf and boar hunting but today it is rare and has degenerated. Height about 23 in. Colours fawn, wheaten, red and white or light grey. Coat of medium length, rough and thick.

Chinese Greyhound (Tschika) This is an elegant coursing hound whose history is rather obscure.

It may have descended from English Greyhounds that had been traded in China by the East India Company. Two sizes are acceptable, the larger being about the size of an English Greyhound and the other smaller than a Whippet. The coat is short and smooth; fawn, cream or brown in colour usually with a white blaze. Ears erect. Tail slightly fringed.

Clydesdale Terrier (Paisley Terrier) Believed to be extinct. Greatly resembled the Skye Terrier.

Cumberland Sheepdog Rare if not extinct. Resembled the Old English working sheepdog although rather larger. Colour black and white.

Deutscher Jagdterrier A German sporting terrier originally produced by crossing the old type of rough-coated Black and Tan Terriers with Wire-haired Fox Terriers.

Dingo (Australian Native Dog; Australian Wild Dog) A primitive canine type believed to have migrated with the aborigines from Asia but is now wild and, owing to its sheep-killing propensities not suitable for domestication. Colour usually reddish or pale fawn—general appearance similar to that of the Spitz family.

Dogue de Bordeaux An ancient Continental fighting breed that has never aroused interest in Britain or the U.S.A. It is uncertain whether it was originally a cross between Mastiffs and the old fighting bulldogs or a descendant of the Alans or Alaunts brought to Europe by the oriental Alains. An excellent guard dog.

Drever (Swedish Dachsbracke) A small, long-cast and short-coated hound with a good nose used for hunting fox, hare and wild boar.

Dropper An old fashioned term for a cross-bred Pointer and Setter.

Dutch Herder One of the national breeds of Holland mainly developed by farmers who value working ability more highly than standardised looks; in consequence appearance is apt to be variable. Coat may be rough, smooth or long. Ears small, pointed and carried erect. Tail of natural length.

English Water Spaniel Now extinct but part ancestor of several sporting breeds. Was once an immensely popular shooting dog especially in East Anglia. The coat was very curly, crisp and dense and usually liver or tan in colour. A peculiarity was the greater height of the hind quarters than the fore quarters, giving an upward sloping backline.

Fila de Terceiro A courageous guard and watch-dog found only on the island of Terceira in the Azores. Bears some resemblance to a Bull-mastiff.

Greek Herder (Spartiate) An ancient breed related to the Kuvasz and much valued by herdsmen and farmers.

Hairless Dogs Various types of hairless dogs are found in Mexico, the West Indies, Africa, China and Turkey. The Mexican variety known as Xoloiscuintli is protected by the Mexican canine ruling body. Specimens were imported into England in 1956 and were exhibited here. There may be some descendants still living. (**See** also Chinese Crested Dogs, p. 38.) The body temperature of these dogs is usually higher than the canine normal.

Happa Dog (Chinese Pug) A mysterious Oriental dog. Theories about its origin and history conflict.

Harlequin Pinscher Similar in outline although slightly larger than the Miniature Pinscher (p. 100). Coat short, smooth and dense and dappled or splashed with black or brindle on a white or pale coloured background.

Havanese **See** Bichon, p. 152.

Iceland Dog This breed has existed in Iceland for centuries and is used for tracking game or stock. These dogs are typical members of the Spitz family with erect ears, thick, medium length coats and a bushy tail curled over the back. The breed has become very uncommon, but there are one or two in England at the present time. Height 12–16 in. Various colours with white markings.

Italian Segugio This is a hound with great powers of endurance who will work either alone or in a pack. Since it would have no place in the English hunting field it is not known in Britain or the U.S.A. although familiar in most Continental countries where it also finds favour as a house dog. The outstanding physical features are the very low-set, triangular and fine textured ears which hang close to the cheeks. The coat is hard, close and dense about 1–2 in. long and maybe black, chestnut-brown, or black, white and tan in colour.

Kabyle Dog   A herding and guard dog of rather primitive type but appreciated in Tunisia and Algeria. Many, however, are simply scavengers following nomadic Arabs and owning no master. Height about 23½ in. Prick ears and long bushy tail. Colour usually white with fawn or red markings.

Kangaroo Dog (Kangaroo Greyhound)   A dog of uncertain ancestry bred in Australia for hunting kangaroo and believed to incorporate the blood of Staghounds, Irish Wolfhounds and Greyhounds. King Edward VII, when Prince of Wales, exhibited a dog of this type in London in 1864. Height about 28 in. Weight 65–80 lb. Coat short and harsh and of almost any colour. These are extremely muscular dogs and very powerful.

Kelpie (Australian Sheepdog)   These dogs combine the blood of the original working collies taken to Australia by settlers with that of the Dingo, and have proved very satisfactory both in Australia and in the U.S.A.

Kerry Beagle   These uncommon hounds are best exemplified in the Scarteen pack owned by the Ryan family of Limerick since 1735. These hounds are larger than the orthodox Beagle and their original forbears were probably the St Hubert Hounds. Height about 23 in. Colour black and tan, blue mottled or blue with white markings. Coat short and somewhat harsh. Body rather long and ears long and pendulous.

Kuri (New Zealand Native Dog; Maori Dog)   It is likely that this typical Spitz breed was imported into New Zealand from the Asiatic mainland in the 14th century by the Maori immigrants from Tahiti and Hawaii.   It seems to have been a mute and indolent dog regarded mainly as the Maori sacrificial tabu or sacred meal.   It was bred mainly for its hair and its meat.   The long tail hairs were used for decorating native spears.   The meat, when eaten by Captain Cook in 1769, was said to resemble fresh killed lamb.   Opinions vary as to whether the breed is now extinct or still exists in small numbers and valued as a watch dog.   Height 13½ in.   Short-haired and prick-eared.   Curled and bushy tail.   Colour white or white with black markings.

Laika   This represents a group of breeds rather than a single race of dog and includes the Ostiak. They vary according to the localities in which they are bred and the purposes for which they are used by the tribes who utilise them.   The Laika is found from Finland to Karelia, the home of the Tongoose and Voguls.   All are typical of the Spitz family.   Average height about 23 in.   Weight around 50 lb.   Colour wolf-grey or fawn with darker shadings.   Coat thick and medium or long. Erect ears and plumed and curled tail.

Leonberger   It is said that Herr Essig wanted to create a dog that resembled the lions depicted on the coat of arms of the town of Leonberg.   With this in view he crossed a St Bernard with a Newfoundland and the progeny with Pyrenean Mountain Dogs.   The results were handsome, strong dogs and a number was bred on the Continent in the first half of the present century.   However, few survived the last war, although shortly afterwards one was brought to England and exhibited at Cruft's. Height 27–30 in. Long, moderately soft coat, neither wavy nor curly but forming a mane on neck and chest. There should be feathering behind the legs. Thick, soft undercoat. Long bushy, pendant tail. Colour golden to reddish, preferably with dark mask. A quiet affectionate companion but a fearless guard.

Leopard Dog This type of dog recently developed in the United States for work with cattle has not as yet been given an official standard or recognition. A powerful, racy dog with a smooth, light coloured coat heavily splashed with dark markings.

Llewellin Setter One of the original strains of what is now called the English Setter (p. 58) and built up by Mr Purcell Llewellin in the 19th century.

Lundehund (Norwegian Puffin Dog) Now a very rare breed but once numerous in north Norway and the Lofoten Islands where it was used for searching in caves and rock crannies for Puffins which were valued for their feathers. The dog's large feet with six toes were of assistance in its work. When it became more usual to work with nets the dogs became rare and during the last war distemper and breeding difficulties nearly wiped them out. Nevertheless, the breed now has a club devoted to its preservation and seems likely to survive. A Spitz breed with erect ears and a thick, double coat usually fox-red or fawn with white markings on neck, chest and feet. Height 9–10 in.

Lurcher   A cross-bred dog usually associated with gypsies and poachers. Greyhound or Whippet blood is generally present in the most sagacious workers, many of which used to come from Norfolk.   The decline in the rabbit population and a change in poaching methods, added to an affluent society has resulted in an increasing lack of interest in what was once a fleet and highly intelligent tyke.

Münsterlander   A Continental gundog which originated in Germany and descended from the old hawking dogs and various spaniels.   The two varieties, Large and Small, are, in fact, separate breeds and not inter-bred.   These dogs are diligent and industrious workers.   A litter was born in English quarantine kennels in May 1971.   The Large Münsterlander stands 23–25 in.   Sleek and slightly wavy white coat with black head and body patches.   The Small Münsterlander stands 18–22 in.   Colour white with brown. Sometimes tan markings on head.

Norfolk Spaniel   Sometimes mentioned by old writers but now extinct as a pure breed although an ancestor of the modern Springer Spaniel.

Owtcharka   This is a widely spread family of Russian herding and guard dogs.   In recent years they have been utilised by the police and army of the U.S.S.R. but little detailed information is available.   There are several regional types and size varies but all have abundant and weather-resisting coats.

Pariah Dog (Pi Dog)   There is no better-known dog in the Orient than that canine outcast the Pariah.   The Pariah is not a breed but a type and is commonly found in the East from Turkey to India and its value is largely as a scavenger. Generally these dogs divide into packs, living on what refuse they can find. Each pack has a leader and seldom intermingles or hunts with other packs. Although not friendly to mankind they seldom attack human beings. The type has created some interest for naturalists in recent years. It is impossible to give a definite description as variations are considerable but usually they resemble their relative the Dingo.

Parson Jack Russell Terrier The Rev. John Russell, M.F.H. (1795–1883) built up a strain of game, wire-haired Fox Terriers who were expected to run with his hounds, go to ground and bolt a fox from the rocky crannies of Exmoor. The strain is now extinct. Attempts were made to revive it about 1925 but without success. John Russell was one of the founder members of the Kennel Club and a noted judge of Fox Terriers. The term 'Jack Russell' is now often incorrectly applied to small terriers of various shapes and sizes.

Phu Quoc A breed from an island in the Gulf of Siam. Like the Rhodesian Ridgebacks these dogs have a ridge of hair along the spine lying in reverse to the main coat.

Pit Bull Terrier (Pit Dog) About the end of the 18th century when bull baiting began to fall out of favour, dog-fighting became the new sport, for which dogs were especially bred. From that time until 1835, when such contests were declared illegal, a breed of Bull Terrier was created which became the forerunner of the present-day Staffordshire Bull Terrier (p. 133). The term Pit Dog was at one time widely used in the U.S.A. for what is now known both in Britain and the U.S.A. as the Staffordshire Bull Terrier.

Plott Hound   This hound has not been given official status by the American Kennel Club although it has been bred in North Carolina for some 200 years.   These hounds were originally taken to the United States by a family of German settlers by the name of Plott.   Valued as a pack hound to hunt wolf, puma, coyote, wild cat, red deer.   Height 21½–23½ in.   Coat short, harsh and close lying.   Colour tan pied with black saddle.

Pocket Beagle (Rabbit Beagle)   This term is now almost exclusively used to refer to historic packs. Small Beagles have been bred for centuries and used for both hares and rabbits.   Queen Elizabeth I had a pack which was carried on horse-back to the hunt.   Queen Victoria's pack of about nine couple averaged only 9–10 in. high; a painting of these by William Barraud was executed in 1844.   Height 9–13½ in.   Except for slightly shorter backs they were exact miniatures of the modern Beagle.

Podhal Polish Herder   (Owczarek Podhalański; Owczarek Tatrzańriski)   The most useful of Polish breeds is the mountain variety of this Sheepdog. Although it is not by any means a common sight in Poland, this dog is used for herding sheep, hauling dairy and bakery carts, guiding the blind and guarding homesteads.   Even the dog's hair combings are made full use of, those of the soft undercoat being woven into clothing and the outer hairs into upholstery.   The breed is mainly found in the Podhal, Tatra, Nowy Targ and Poronin districts. Height 25–27 in.   Weight 75–90 lb.   Colour

white or cream.   Body coat thick and profuse and
slightly wavy; on head and muzzle soft and smooth.
Low-set tail, well covered in hair and reaching to
the hocks.

Polish Lowland Herder (Owczarek Nizinny)   A
small to medium-sized long-coated dog whose tail
is often docked.   There are three varieties varying
only in size.   The smaller type are more active but
all are untiring workers and very hardy.   The
thick abundant coat is over 4 in. long and shaggy
with hair almost obscuring the eyes.   Colours
various.

Pomeranian Sheepdog (Pommerscher Huet-
hund)   The modern and accepted ideal of the
Bodenstaendige Huethunden, the group of native
shepherd dogs of old Pomerania, is the Pomeranian
Sheepdog proper—an all white breed rather like
the Maremmani (p. 98).   The race has long been
of valuable assistance to the shepherds of the
undulating country of north-east Germany.   A
few of these dogs were imported into England in
1938 and were very favourably received but the
War made progress difficult.   For some time
descendants of these importations were working
on a Devonshire farm.   Height 21–23 in.   Weight
50–60 lb.   Colour white with or without lemon or
fawn head markings.   Coat medium in length and
soft in texture.   The head has a slight stop and
tapers to a fine muzzle; ears semi-erect, small and
triangular.   Tail long and low set.

Portuguese Cattle Dog   These dogs are of
Mastiff type and a very ancient breed highly
thought of as watch and guard dogs.   Height
23–27 in.   Weight 90–110 lb.   The hair resembles

that of a goat but may be either short or long. The small, triangular ears are sometimes cropped. Tail thick and well covered with hair; sometimes docked. Colour red with black mask most usual, sometimes grey or pied.

Portuguese Pointer (Perdigeiro) The Portuguese Pointer is not as beautiful as the English Pointer but he is a capable and reliable worker. These dogs are used with the gun for almost all types of game and are becoming increasingly popular. The shortened tail is unusual amongst pointing breeds. The breed has a club taking an active interest in its development. Height 26–29½ in. Weight 55–60 lb. Coat short and smooth with no undercoat. Whole coloured brown, white, fawn, red or black or with one of these colours patched on a white ground.

Portuguese Sheepdog These dogs are used almost entirely for the protection of flocks. Independent, massive and inclined to be ferocious, they are not often exhibited at shows. Height 25–26½ in. Colour black and tan, tan, tan and red, grey or fawn. Plumed tail reaching to the hocks.

Portuguese Water Dog (Cão d'Agua) This breed is extremely old and greatly valued by the fishing populace. The breed is now confined to the southern shores of the Algarve region but was once common to the entire coast. These excellent water dogs are used for many purposes such as retrieving lost tackle, broken nets and as couriers between ships or the shore. A few years ago two or three specimens appeared at English shows and attracted a good deal of attention but did not make any permanent impact. Height 21¼ in. Weight 46 lb. Colour black, black and white, chocolate, chocolate and white or pearl-grey. Coat long and free, often clipped Poodle fashion with a top-knot and a lion tuft on the tail tip.

Pumi (Hungarian Cattle Dog)   For centuries this breed has been raised solely as a drover of cattle and swine.   Occasionally it is confused with, and regarded as, a variety of the Puli (p. 117) which is quite a different breed with similar origins.   The Pumi is rather wild and headstrong, though quite adaptable and faithful.   In polite circles it is referred to as the shepherd's dog, no distinction being made between Pumi and Puli except in rural areas.   Height 16–18 in.   Weight 18–23 lb. Colour red, black, red-brindle and light brindle; white severely penalised.   Coat harsh and fairly short though covering the eyes; muzzle bearded; ears semi-erect; tail short.

Pyrenean Sheepdog (Berger des Pyrénées)   This is quite a different race to the Pyrenean Mountain Dog (p. 118) with whom it should not be confused. Type varies considerably in different districts with variations in coat colour and ear and tail carriage, but all have large bear-like heads.   An excellent herder of sheep and drover of cattle.   Height 18–20 in.   Colour fawn brindle or grey, often with white.

Rumanian Herder   These are large, strong dogs with long coats, and are highly thought of by the herdsmen to whom they are faithful companions and keen protectors of their herds.   Generally very suspicious of strangers.   Type varies a great deal but these dogs generally stand about 24 in., have strong muzzles, broad skulls, and their medium-length tails are well covered in hair and carried low. Colour usually wolf-grey with lighter undercoat.

Rampur Hound   A powerful hound of the Greyhound type.   Very little information is available about the position today although it was once a familiar sight in north-west India.

St Hubert Hound   There are few hounds in Western Europe that do not contain the blood of the St Hubert Hound, particularly those with long bodies, heavy bone and good scenting ability. This breed was named after the patron saint of hunting, St Hubert (A.D. 656–727), who founded the monastery in the Ardennes where such hounds were bred for several centuries.   Height about 22 in.   Colour black, black with red markings and black with tan eye-spots.

Scottish Spaniel   Now extinct.   A relative of the Irish Setter.   Colour white with red flecks.

Shan Dog   Another name for the smooth-coated Chow Chow (p. 39).

Shock Dog   The Shock Dog was first mentioned by Dr Caius in the 16th century but did not become popular until the 18th century when it was fashionable to be seen in society with one or more of these little dogs.   Probably akin to the Maltese. Height about 12 in.   Weight about 14 lb.   Colour white, or with black or red markings.   Coat soft and curly, with top-knot.

Spanish Pointer (Perdiguero Burgales)   A large, capable and massively built Pointer.   This rather slow but reliable Pointer was the ancestor of the more active and graceful English Pointer. The Spanish breed, although not as popular as it used to be, is often seen in Southern Spain. Height 26–29½ in. Weight 55–65 lb. Coat short and smooth; tail docked. Colour liver and white, or white with liver flecks.

Spinone This is an Italian gundog breed. The modern tendency to develop an all-round dog at the expense of the specialists has been responsible for a revival of interest in the Spinone which is a well-established Italian shooting dog. Accepted by the Italian Kennel Club. At one time there were one or two specimens in England. A sturdily built dog weighing 70–80 lb. Height 23–27½ in. Ears long and tail docked. Coat hard, thick and from 1½ to 2 in. long, shorter on limbs, head and ears but long on cheeks, jaws and eyebrows. Colour white or white with orange or brown markings.

Staghound Ever since the Norman invasion stag hunting has been a popular sport in the New Forest and the moors of south-west England where packs of a large type of hound have been employed for finding and chasing the stag. The Staghound is descended from the old Southern Hound and is larger than the Foxhound although much of the latter's blood has been introduced into the breed. Height dogs 24 in., bitches 22 in. Weight 75 lb. Colour generally that of the Foxhound. (**See** English Foxhound, p. 57.)

Stövare (Swedish Hounds) Sweden is the home of several breeds of small hounds most of them carrying the blood of English Foxhounds or

Beagles. One of the most popular is the Hamilton Stövare, a black and brown hound standing about 21 in. and used for hunting various sorts of game. The Schiller Stövare is slightly smaller and black and tan in colour and used for hunting hare and fox or for tracking. The Småland Stövare is mostly found in Central Sweden and is smaller than the others and also black and tan in colour. A useful hunter of foxes and hares as well as being a companionable house dog.

Swiss Hounds The national hounds of Switzerland are divided into many types, some of them having been crossed with Dachshunds in order to reduce height. Types vary in the different cantons. The maximum height is about 18 in. but more often around 12 in. Type of coat and colours vary.

Tesem (Egyptian Hunting Dog) The prick-eared hunting dog often depicted on Egyptian tombs dating back 4000–5000 years. Possibly the ancestor of some breeds known today.

Tibetan Mastiff A breed of great antiquity and akin to the early mastiffs. Since these dogs have long been used as guardians of the Tibetan monasteries they are apt to be aggressive and resentful of discipline. This, combined with the fact that they are extremely powerful animals, has resulted in efforts to import and domesticate them ending in failure. Height 24½–27½ in. Weight about 165 lb. A large, tremendously strong and heavily boned dog with a massive head, strong blunt muzzle, long coat and a bushy tail carried over the back. Colour black, black and tan or golden.

Tosa (Japanese Fighting Dog; Japanese Mastiff)
The Tosa has been known for at least six centuries
though it does not appear to have been bred with
any care and it has remained fundamentally a
Mastiff type. Since organised dog fighting has
greatly decreased the survival of these dogs seems
doubtful. Height about 24 in. Weight 75–90 lb.
Colour black, tan or brindle. Coat short. Tail
long and set low.

Turnspit (Kitchen Dog; Vernepator) Although
now extinct the Turnspits were for several centuries a common sight in the kitchens of Britain—
in fact until the 19th century when roasting spits
became obsolete. Their duty, often cruelly stimu-
lated, was to 'treadmill' a wheel attached to the spit
while enclosed in a cage. Dr Caius (1570) classified
the Turnspit as a mongrel but Buffon included it
in the hound group. There is no proof of the
suggestion that it was the ancestor of the Dachshund
although short legs and a long body were desirable.
Height about 10 in. Weight about 14 lb. Coat
short.

Ukrainian Sheepdog The Ukrainian Sheepdog
is well known in Russia today where it is being
absorbed into the military machinery as an army
messenger. However, in the Ukraine proper it is
still the common shepherd's dog. It is similar,
and related, to the Hungarian Komondor. Height
about 24 in. Weight about 65 lb. Colour white.
Coat long, rough and thick with woolly undercoat
and long fore-lock. Ears long, tail plumed and
carried gaily.

Vendéen Hound French hounds have been so
inter-bred that, like many others, the pure Vendéen

hound has become extinct, although today a few good Griffons Vendéens are still used for boar and hare in the Vendéen Department. The modern hound is some 3 in. lower at the shoulder than the original. It is closely related to the Welsh Hound through the Chien Fauve de Bretagne. Height 19–22 in. Colour hare or badger pied, fawn and white, with lemon or fawn markings.

Volpino (Volpino Italiano) This is a small white Spitz dog greatly resembling the dogs depicted on old Roman Etruscan pottery. Nowadays an energetic guardian of farms and vineyards, often travelling with the wine casks on their journey to the town. Height 11 in. Weight about 9 lb. Ears erect, long and pointed. Coat profuse and silky with thick undercoat. Colour white.

Welsh Sheepdog (Bugeilgi; Welsh Collie) This type of sheepdog is found in North Wales and descends from the Black and Tan Welsh Collie and the Working Collie. Height about 18 in. Weight approximately 35 lb. Colour black and tan, tricolour, all black or black with white blaze, collar, brisket and underside. Coat fairly long, smooth and close to resist the rain.

Wire-haired Pointing Griffon This is a slow-working and deliberate all-purpose gundog and a comparatively modern production by E. K. Korthals who began his breeding efforts in Holland around 1874 and continued them in Germany. Many breeds have been mentioned as having participated in the foundation of this breed —Pointers, Setters and Otterhounds to name a few. Attempts were made to popularise the breed in England at the end of the last century without permanent success. Some years later it appeared in the U.S.A. where it is now accepted by the American Kennel Club.

Height $21\frac{1}{2}$ to $23\frac{1}{2}$ in. for dogs and less for bitches. A short backed, rather low on the leg dog giving an impression of strength and vigour. Coat as harsh as the bristles of a wild boar. Head long with harsh hair forming a moustache and eyebrows. Ears set high but falling flat. Tail docked to a third. Colour steel grey or greyish white with chestnut splashes, chestnut but never black.

List of breeds, in Groups, Granted Championship Status by the English Kennel Club

Utility Group

Boston Terriers
Bulldogs
Chow Chows
Dalmatians
French Bulldogs
Keeshonds
Lhasa Apsos
Poodles (Standard)
Poodles (Miniature)
Poodles (Toy)
Schipperkes
Schnauzers
Miniature Schnauzers
Shih Tzus
Tibetan Spaniels
Tibetan Terriers

Working Group

Alsatians (German Shepherd Dogs)
Bearded Collies
Boxers
Bullmastiffs
Collies (Rough)
Collies (Smooth)
Dobermanns
Great Danes
Groenendael
Mastiffs
Newfoundlands
Norwegian Buhunds
Old English Sheepdogs

Pyrenean Mountain Dogs
Rottweilers
St Bernards
Samoyeds
Shetland Sheepdogs
Welsh Corgis (Cardigan)
Welsh Corgis (Pembroke)

Toy Group

Chihuahuas (Long Coat)
Chihuahuas (Smooth Coat)
English Toy Terrier (Black and Tan)
Griffons Bruxellois
Italian Greyhounds
Japanese Chin
King Charles Spaniels
Cavalier King Charles Spaniels
Maltese
Miniature Pinschers
Papillons
Pekingese
Pomeranians
Pugs
Yorkshire Terriers

Hound Group

Afghan Hounds
Basenjis
Basset Hounds

Beagles
Bloodhounds
Borzois
Dachshunds (Long-haired)
   (Miniature Long-haired)
   (Smooth-haired)
   (Miniature Smooth-
     haired)
   (Wire-haired)
   (Miniature Wire-haired)
Deerhounds
Elkhounds
Finnish Spitz
Foxhounds
Greyhounds
Irish Wolfhounds
Rhodesian Ridgebacks
Whippets

Gundog Group

English Setters
Gordon Setters
Irish Setters (Red)
Pointers
German Shorthaired
   Pointers
Retrievers (Curly-coated)
   (Flat-coated)
   (Golden)
   (Labrador)
Spaniels (American Cocker)
   (Clumber)

   (Cocker)
   (Field)
   (Irish Water)
   (Springer, English)
   (Springer, Welsh)
   (Sussex)
Weimaraners

Terrier Group

Airedale Terriers
Australian Terriers
Bedlington Terriers
Border Terriers
Bull Terriers
Bull Terriers (Miniature)
Cairn Terriers
Dandie Dinmont Terriers
Fox Terriers (Smooth)
   (Wire)
Irish Terriers
Kerry Blue Terriers
Lakeland Terriers
Manchester Terriers
Norfolk Terriers
Norwich Terriers
Scottish Terriers
Sealyham Terriers
Skye Terriers
Staffordshire Bull Terriers
Welsh Terriers
West Highland White
   Terriers

List of Breeds, in Groups, as Accepted by the American Kennel Club

Group I Sporting Dogs

Pointer
Pointer, German
    Short-haired
Pointer, German
    Wire-haired
Retriever, Chesapeake Bay
Retriever, Curly-coated
Retriever, Flat-coated
Retriever, Golden
Retriever, Labrador
Setter, English
Setter, Gordon
Setter, Irish
Spaniel, American Water
Spaniel, Brittany
Spaniel, Clumber
Spaniel, Cocker
Spaniel, English Cocker
Spaniel, English Springer
Spaniel, Field
Spaniel, Irish Water
Spaniel, Sussex
Spaniel, Welsh Springer
Vizsla
Weimaraner
Wire-haired Pointing
    Griffon

Group II Hounds

Afghan Hound
Basenji
Basset Hound
Beagle
Black and Tan Coonhound
Bloodhound
Borzoi
Dachshund
Foxhound, American
Foxhound, English
Greyhound
Harrier
Irish Wolfhound
Norwegian Elkhound
Otterhound
Rhodesian Ridgeback
Saluki
Scottish Deerhound
Whippet

Group III Working Dogs

Alaskan Malamute
Belgian Malinois
Belgian Sheepdog
Belgian Tervuren
Bernese Mountain Dog
Bouvier des Flandres
Boxer
Briard
Bullmastiff
Collie
Dobermann Pinscher
German Shepherd Dog
Giant Schnauzer

Great Dane
Great Pyrenees
Komondor
Kuvasz
Mastiff
Newfoundland
Old English Sheepdog
Puli
Rottweiler
St Bernard
Samoyed
Shetland Sheepdog
Siberian Husky
Standard Schnauzer
Welsh Corgi, Cardigan
Welsh Corgi, Pembroke

Group IV   Terriers

Airedale Terrier
Australian Terrier
Bedlington Terrier
Border Terrier
Bull Terrier
Cairn Terrier
Dandie Dinmont Terrier
Fox Terrier
Irish Terrier
Kerry Blue Terrier
Lakeland Terrier
Manchester Terrier
Miniature Schnauzer
Norwich Terrier
Scottish Terrier
Sealyham Terrier
Skye Terrier
Staffordshire Terrier

Welsh Terrier
West Highland White
   Terrier

Group V   Toys

Affenpinscher
Brussels Griffon
Chihuahua
English Toy Spaniel
Italian Greyhound
Japanese Spaniel
Maltese
Manchester Terrier (Toy)
Miniature Pinscher
Papillon
Pekingese
Pomeranian
Poodle (Toy)
Pug
Shih Tzu
Silky Terrier
Yorkshire Terrier

Group VI   Non-sporting Dogs

Boston Terrier
Bulldog
Chow Chow
Dalmatian
French Bulldog
Keeshond
Lhasa Apso
Poodle
Schipperke

Metric Conversion Table

Height		Weight	
Inches	*Centimetres*	*Pounds*	*Kilograms*
1	2·54	1	0·454
2	5·08	2	0·907
3	7·62	3	1·361
4	10·16	4	1·814
5	12·70	5	2·268
6	15·24	6	2·722
7	17·78	7	3·175
8	20·32	8	3·629
9	22·86	9	4·082
10	25·40	10	4·536
11	27·94	11	4·989
12	30·48	12	5·443
13	33·02	13	5·897
14	35·56	14	6·350
15	38·10	15	6·804
16	40·64	16	7·257
17	43·18	17	7·711
18	45·72	18	8·165
19	48·26	19	8·618
20	50·80	20	9·072
21	53·34	30	13·608
22	55·88	40	18·144
23	58·42	50	22·680
24	60·96	60	27·216
25	63·50	70	31·751
26	66·04	80	36·287
27	68·58	90	40·823
28	71·12	100	45·359
29	73·66	110	49·895
30	76·20	120	54·431
31	78·74	130	58·967
32	81·28	140	63·503
33	83·82	150	68·039
34	86·36	200	90·718

Winners of award for 'Best in Show' at Cruft's
1928–1972

Year	Dog's Name	Breed	Sex	Owner	Breeder
1928	Ch. Primley Sceptre	Greyhound	B	Mr H. Whitley	Owner
1929	Ch. Heather Necessity	Scottish Terrier	D	Mr R. Chapman	Mr Walker
1930	Luckystar of Ware	Cocker Spaniel	D	Mr H. S. Lloyd	Mr Ottley
1931	Luckystar of Ware	Cocker Spaniel	D	Mr H. S. Lloyd	Mr Ottley
1932	Ch. and F.T. Ch. Bramshaw Bob	Labrador Retriever	D	Lorna, Countess Howe	Sir George Bullough
1933	Ch. and F.T. Ch. Bramshaw Bob	Labrador Retriever	D	Lorna, Countess Howe	Sir George Bullough
1934	Ch. Southball Moonstone	Greyhound	B	Mr B. Hartland-Worden	Owner
1935	Pennine Prima Donna	Pointer	B	Mr A. Eggleston	
1936	Ch. Choonam Hung Kwong	Chow Chow	D	Mrs Mannooch	Owner
1937	Ch. Cheverells Ben of Banchory	Labrador Retriever	D	Lorna, Countess Howe	Mr R. G. Heaton
1938	Exquisite Model of Ware	Cocker Spaniel	B	Mr H. S. Lloyd	Mr C. C. D. Youings

179

Year	Dog's Name	Breed	Sex	Owner	Breeder
1939	Exquisite Model of Ware	Cocker Spaniel	B	Mr H. S. Lloyd	Mr C. C. D. Youings
1940–1947	Not held				
1948	Tracey Witch of Ware	Cocker Spaniel	B	Mr H. S. Lloyd	Miss D. Weldon
1949	Not held				
1950	Tracey Witch of Ware	Cocker Spaniel	B	Mr H. S. Lloyd	Miss D. Weldon
1951	Ch. Twynstar Dyma-Fi	Welsh Terrier	B	Capt. and Mrs Thomas	Mr T. M. Jones
1952	Ch. Noways Chuckles	Bulldog	B	Mr J. Barnard	Owner
1953	Ch. Elch Edler of Ouborough	Great Dane	D	Mr W. G. Siggers	Mr J. V. Rank
1954	Not held				
1955	Ch. Tzigane Aggri of Nashend	Poodle	D	Mrs Proctor	Owner
1956	Ch. Treetops Golden Falcon	Greyhound	D	Mrs de Casembroot and Miss H. Greenish	Owners
1957	Ch. Volkrijk of Vorden	Keeshond	B	Mrs I. Tucker	Owner
1958	Ch. Chiming Bells	Pointer	B	Mrs Parkinson	Mrs M. Bowman

Year	Dog's Name	Breed	Sex	Owner	Breeder
1959	Ch. Sandstorm Saracen	Welsh Terrier	D	Mrs M. M. Thomas and Mrs D. M. Leach	Mrs E. M. Russell
1960	Ch. Sulhampstead Merman	Irish Wolfhound	D	Mrs F. Nagle and Miss M. Clarke	Owners
1961	Ch. Riverina Tweedsbairn	Airedale Terrier	D	Miss P. McCaughey and Mrs D. Schuth	Mrs C. M. Halford
1962	Ch. Crackwyn Cockspur	Fox Terrier (Wire)	D	Mr H. L. Gill	Owner
1963	Ch. Rogerholme Recruit	Lakeland Terrier	D	Mr B. Rogers	Major Horseman
1964	Sh. Ch. Silbury Soames of Madavale	English Setter	D	Mrs A. W. Williams	Mr and Mrs Gardiner-Swann
1965	Ch. Fenton of Kentwood	Alsatian (G.S.D.)	D	Miss S. H. Godden	Owner
1966	Ch. Oakington Puckshill Amber Sunblush	Poodle (Toy)	B	Mrs C. E. Perry	Mrs Dobson
1967	Ch. Stingray of Derryabah	Lakeland Terrier	D	Mr and Mrs Postlethwaite	Owners

181

Year	Dog's Name	Breed	Sex	Owner	Breeder
1968	Ch. Fanhill Faune	Dalmatian	B	Mrs E. J. Woodyatt	Owner
1969	Hendrawen's Nibelung of Charavigne	Alsatian (G.S.D.)	D	Mr and Mrs E. J. White	Mrs I. Dummett
1970	Bergerie Knur	Pyrenean Mountain Dog	D	Mr and Mrs F. S. Prince	Miss P. M. Grant-Dalton
1971	Ramacon Swashbuckler	Alsatian (G.S.D.)	D	Prince Ahmed Husain	Mr W. Rankin
1972	Ch. Abraxas Audacity	Bull Terrier	D	Miss V. Drummond-Dick	Owner

182

Glossary of Technical Terms

Action Movement.

A.K.C. American Kennel Club.

Apple Head Rounded or domed skull—a virtue in some breeds such as Chihuahuas, but a fault in others.

Beard The very profuse and bushy whiskers of the Griffon Bruxellois, quite distinct from Terrier whiskers.

Belton The lemon- or blue-flecked colour of certain English Setters, notably the Laverack strain.

B.I.S. Abbreviation often used for 'Best in Show'.

Bitch A female dog.

Blaze An attractive narrow or bulbous-shaped white marking running up the face between the eyes.

B.O.B. Abbreviation for Best of Breed.

Bone A well-boned dog is one possessing limbs giving an appearance and feel of strength and spring without coarseness.

Breeching Tan markings at the back of the thighs of a black and tan dog such as the Gordon Setter.

Brindle A mixture of light and dark hairs, usually darker streaks on a grey, tawny or brown background.

Brush Term applied to a bushy tail similar to that of the fox.

Cat-feet Short, compact and round feet common to Terriers, and opposed to splay-feet.

Challenge Certificate (C.C.) Award given, at judge's discretion, to best of sex of breed at some major English shows.

Champion In England a dog that has won three Challenge Certificates under three different judges at shows of championship status. In the U.S.A. the title is awarded on points won at major shows.

Chops Pendulous upper lips or flews common to the Bulldog, some hounds and most deep-mouthed dogs.

Cobby Well ribbed and sprung, rather short in back, adequately muscled and compact.

Couplings The length of the body between last rib and pelvis.

Cropped In some breeds the ears are cropped or cut to erect shapes. It is unacceptable in Britain and some American States.

Croup The region adjacent to the sacrum and immediately anterior to the set-on or root of the tail.

Cryptorchid An adult dog whose testicles have not descended into scrotum. This condition bars a dog from exhibition.

Culotte   The feathery hair on the backs of the legs, as seen on the Pomeranian.

Cushion   That appearance of swelling or padding given by the full upper lips of the Mastiff and Bulldog.

Dew-claw   A claw often found on the inside of the leg and usually removed early in life but retained by some mountain breeds.

Dish-faced   A term used to describe a concavity in the nasal bone making the nose-tip higher than the stop.

Docked   Many breeds have their tails docked or cut short to specially designed lengths when quite young.

Down-faced   When the nose-tip is well below the level of the stop, due to a downward inclination of the nasal bone.

Drop-eared   When the ears are pendant and hanging close and flat to the side of the cheeks.

Entropion   A condition where the eyelid turns inward and the lashes irritate the eyeball.

Fall   Long hair overhanging the face.

Featherings   Those long and fine fringes of hair seen on the backs of legs in Setters, Spaniels and some Sheepdogs.

Flag   The fringe or feather found under the tails of Setters and some Retrievers, long at the base and shorter at the tip.

Flecked   When the coat is lightly ticked with other colours, as in the English Setter, and neither roaned nor spotted.

Flews   Deep, hanging upper lips.

Fly-eared   Usually a blemish, in that ears which should be erect fall or tilt at the tips.

Frill   That long feathering of soft hair found on Setters and Collies around the neck and longer at the throat and base.

Fringes   A loosely applied term usually meaning the featherings of long-coated breeds. (*See* Featherings.)

Gay   A tail is said to be gay when it is curled up over the back or erect as in some hounds.

Gazehound   Greyhound or hound that hunts by sight.

Hare-feet   Such feet as have the digits well separated, usually being long, like a hare's.

Haw   The inner part of the lower eyelid which shows red and hangs open in such breeds as the St Bernard and Bloodhound.

Hip Dysphasia   Abnormal development of the bones of the hip joint.   Found in several breeds.   Usually hereditary.

Hocks   Those joints in the hind limbs below the true knees, or stifle-joints.

Hound-marked   Fox Terriers are described as hound-marked when their body patches conform to the pattern of hound markings.

Leather   The flap of the ear.   The term has particular reference to ears which are pendant and large.

Mask   The muzzle or fore-face, generally so-called with reference to colour: for example, a light Cairn may have a dark mask.

Merle   A blue-grey mixture streaked or ticked with black, and usually seen in some Collies and Shetland Sheepdogs.

Over Nose Wrinkle   A fold of loose skin dropping forward from the skull on to the bridge of the nose.   Seen in Pugs, Pekingese and some other short-nosed breeds.

Over-shot   When the upper teeth project beyond the lower.   A blemish in most breeds, though the lesser of jaw malformations.

Parti-colour   A term used for dogs of two colours *in equal proportion*, usually red and white and black and white.

Patella Luxation   The knee cap or stifle slips or dislocates.   An abnormality said to be hereditary and found in several small breeds.

Peak   The pronounced and pointed top of the occiput which is, in the Bloodhound and allied breeds, a favourable point.

Pencillings   The dark and elegant lines on the surface of the toes in some breeds, notably the English Toy Terrier.

Pied   When two colours occur in irregular patches, one more than the other, a dog is said to be pied.

Plumes   Whereas the brush is not always soft, plumes refer to the soft hair on the tail of the Pekingese and Pomeranian.

Prick-eared   When the ears are erect, as in Chow Chows, Schipperkes, Alsatians and Welsh Corgis.

Progressive Retinal Atrophy (P.R.A.)   Sometimes incorrectly called 'night blindness'.   This is a hereditary defect of the eyes found in several breeds causing early loss of sight.

Puppy   A dog under a year old.

Roached   A dog's back is roached when it arches convexly, as in the Dandie Dinmont, Italian Greyhound and Whippet.

Roan   A mixture of coloured hair with white hair as in many Cocker Spaniels—blue-roan, liver-roan, orange-roan, etc.

Rose-eared   When the ear, neither pricked nor dropped, folds or twists over, showing the inside, as in the Bulldog.

Ruff   The stand-off frill or apron of long (usually coarse) hair around the neck, as in the Chow Chow.

Saddle   The black rectangular marking on the back extending to the upper flanks, as in the Airedale and Welsh Terriers.

Self-marked   A dog is so-called when it is a whole colour, with white or pale markings on the chest, feet and tail-tip.

Slipping Stifle   *See* patella luxation.

Splay-feet   Feet of which the toes are spread out, as in some sporting breeds used in water-fowling.

GLOSSARY OF TECHNICAL TERMS

Stern A term frequently employed for the tail, with particular reference to Foxhounds, Harriers and Beagles.

Stifle That joint in the hind leg of a dog most approximating to the knee in man, particularly relating to the inner side.

Stop The depression between and in front of the eyes roughly corresponding to the bridge of the nose.

Tongue To 'give tongue' is for a Hound to voice when on the scent. To 'sing', being a moderate tongue, and 'babble', an excess.

Top-knot The longer, finer hair on the top of the head rather like a powder-puff, as in Dandie Dinmonts.

Tricolour A term used when dogs have three colours more or less proportionate, usually black, tan and white, as in hounds.

Trousers The hair on the hind-quarters. The term is often used in reference to Afghan Hounds and Poodles.

Tucked-up When the loins are lifted up yet the chest is deep, giving a racy appearance, as in Borzoi, Greyhounds and Whippets.

Undercoat That soft furry wool beneath the outer hair of some breeds, giving protection against cold and wet.

Under-shot When the lower jaw and teeth project beyond the upper, as in the Bulldog and allied races.

Wall eyes Eyes parti-coloured white and blue, seen in merle-coloured Collies and Sheepdogs, often keenly valued.

Whiskers The beard of Fox Terriers and allied Terriers, generally elongated and tidy, rather than bushy and too profuse.

Wrinkle The loose folds of skin puckered up on the brow and sides of the face in Bloodhounds, St Bernards and Basenjis, Pugs, etc.

Index to Breeds

187

INDEX TO BREEDS

NOTES

NOTES

NOTES

NOTES

NOTES

NOTES

NOTES

NOTES